Designing
Furniture

Designing
Furniture

The Editors of
Fine Woodworking

The Taunton Press

The Taunton Press
Inspiration for hands-on living®

The Taunton Press, Inc., 63 South Main Street, PO Box 5506, Newtown, CT 06470-5506
e-mail: tp@taunton.com

Distributed by Publishers Group West

Jacket/Cover design: Susan Fazekas
Interior design and layout: Susan Fazekas

Front Cover Photographer: Jonathan Binzen
Back Cover Photographers: (clockwise from top left) Jonathan Binzen, courtesy of *Fine Woodworking,* © The Taunton Press, Inc.; Strother Purdy, courtesy of *Fine Woodworking,* © The Taunton Press, Inc.; Asa Christiana, courtesy of *Fine Woodworking,* © The Taunton Press, Inc.

Fine Woodworking® is a trademark of The Taunton Press, Inc., registered in the U.S. Patent and Trademark Office.

Library of Congress Cataloging-in-Publication Data

Designing furniture / the editors of Fine woodworking.
     p. cm. -- (The new best of fine woodworking)
 ISBN 1-56158-684-6
 1. Furniture design. I. Fine woodworking. II. Series.
 TT196.D47 2004
 684.1'04--dc22

                              2003017122

Printed in the United States of America
10 9 8 7 6 5 4 3 2

The following manufacturers/names appearing in *Designing Furniture* are trademarks:
3M®, Delta®, Ebon-X™, Elmer's®, Masonite®, Pantone®, Surform®

Working wood is inherently dangerous. Using hand or power tools improperly or ignoring safety practices can lead to permanent injury or even death. Don't try to perform operations you learn about here (or elsewhere) unless you're certain they are safe for you. If something about an operation doesn't feel right, don't do it. Look for another way. We want you to enjoy the craft, so please keep safety foremost in your mind whenever you're in the shop.

Acknowledgments

Special thanks to the authors, editors, art directors, copy editors, and other staff members of *Fine Woodworking* who contributed to the development of the articles in this book.

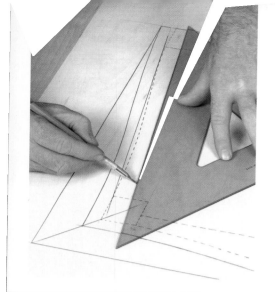

Contents

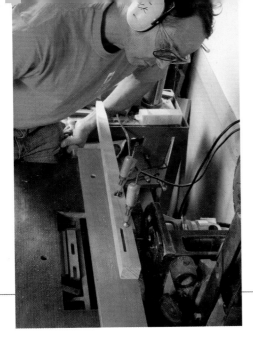
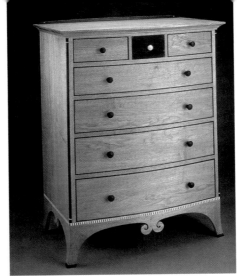
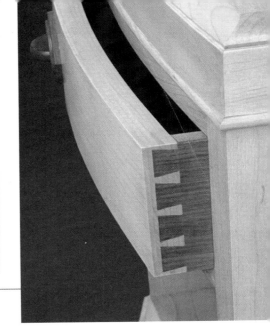

Introduction

There is something wonderful about turning a rough idea into a well-crafted, pleasing and useful piece of furniture. The successful furniture makers find a way to tie the piece together with little consistent details. They expertly craft the way the horizontal surfaces meet and compliment the vertical lines and parts.

Their eyes and minds give them the proportions that make the piece of furniture feel grounded and statuesque at the same time.

But it doesn't just happen — at least not for most of us. Every woodworker should save his or her first original project, just as a reminder of how far they've come. My greatest furniture-making disaster is also the only piece I've ever sold. It was a svelte but pitiful wall rack for displaying plates. The shelves were too small, the joinery was ugly and the finish was not finished. But some needy soul took pity on it and its $5 price tag at our yard sale.

My second, and much more original, project is still in our house, although it's been relegated to the basement guest room. Now, when guests remark on the crude, pine coffee table, I joke that my blind grandfather made it. My ego doesn't suffer because I assume they've seen the subsequent furniture projects were good enough to bring up from the basement.

I've learned a great deal about furniture design in the years since that coffee table took shape. Much of it I learned from the woodworkers who have written the chapters of this book, because many have been

sharing their secrets in the pages of *Fine Woodworking* magazine for years.

In the chapters that follow, you'll find guidance on furniture styles such as Arts & Crafts and Shaker. You'll learn about developing your sense of aesthetic design and the correct approaches to construction design.

The Taunton Press editors of this book searched the issues of *Fine Woodworking* magazine to find the best articles about

designing furniture. The advice from our experienced authors will surely improve your appreciation for all fine furniture design. And if your woodworking projects are already good enough to bring up from the basement, you'll undoubtedly find that your future work will be even better than what you've already put on display.

—Tim Schreiner, publisher of *Fine Woodworking*

A Short History of Design

BY GRAHAM
BLACKBURN

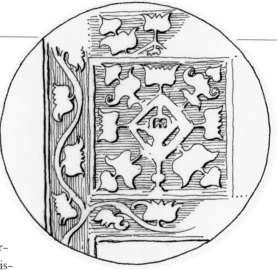

SINCE *FINE WOODWORKING'S* inception 27 years ago, a vast range of furniture from various periods has appeared in its pages. What follows is a condensed overview describing many of these various styles. I've tried to put them into a historical perspective based on their defining characteristics, but the process of design is continual and unending. Hepplewhite and Sheraton styles, for instance, were made during the Mahogany Period in England but weren't prevalent in the United States until after the Revolution, during the Federal Period.

Any attempt to categorize definitively the products of a given period is bound to be inexact. It is in the very nature of furniture design to evolve, often haphazardly, taking a little from here and a little from there, sometimes making a large leap with the invention of a new technique or a new material.

British furniture is most often described in terms of the various monarchs during whose reigns it was made, but for a more familiar division of furniture design in America, I've chosen more local names. Nevertheless, it remains true that most American furniture is very similar to the contemporaneous British styles. A great deal of furniture from the early periods made in the United States was built by craftsmen either trained in Britain or who used British patterns. By the 20th century the differences had more to do with individual makers than with national styles.

GRAHAM BLACKBURN is a furniture maker, author, illustrator and the publisher of Blackburn Books (www.blackburnbooks.com).

It is in the very nature of furniture design to evolve, …taking a little from here and a little from there, sometimes making a large leap with . . . a new technique or a new material.

The Pilgrim Century, 1620-1750

Much early American furniture came here with the first immigrants, including, most famously, the Pilgrims. They brought—and then made—oak pieces typical of the Jacobean, William and Mary, and Carolean periods in Britain; pieces that retained a strong Gothic influence, sturdy pieces, heavily carved pieces, pieces with cup-turned legs and bun feet. Much of the work from this Early Colonial Period is representative of a utilitarian life.

The Elder Brewster Chair, ca. 1650

- Wainscot constructed oak (wainscot means "wagon oak" and refers to the paneling)
- Joiner's work
- Framed construction, pinned for strength
- Bold turnings
- Heavily carved
- Stout stretchers
- Less-heavily carved chairs of the same construction are common
- Reminiscent of earlier British chairs in the Gothic style

The Nicholas Disbrowe Chest, 1660

- Nicholas Disbrowe is the first known American maker
- Oak, frame-and-panel construction
- Uncompromisingly rectangular
- Similar to earlier English oak styles, but distinctive Connecticut Valley, Hadley style
- This piece shows the chest becoming a chest of drawers
- Tulip motif carved over entire foot

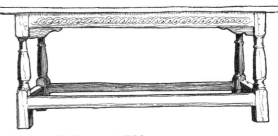

Dining Table, ca. 1700

- Oak
- Strap carving on front apron
- Simple turning with square ends on legs
- Stout stretchers
- Edge-joined top
- Pinned mortise-and-tenon construction
- Bracketed legs
- Post-assembly carving (as on old chests)

"Bible" Box, 1670

- As with most boxes of the period, this one is nailed together
- Oak throughout, but many boxes were made of pine or with top and bottom of pine
- Lunette and flute carvings were simple and geometrically based
- Overhanging, cleated top

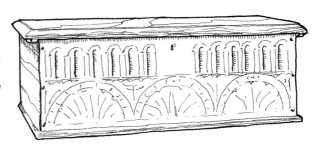

The Mahogany Period, 1702-1780

The Mahogany Period (late Colonial), covering the first half of the 18th century, roughly parallels the periods known in Britain as Queen Anne and Georgian. Walnut gave way to mahogany as the predominant wood, and the beginning of the period saw a sudden simplification of style into a less ornamented and more severely elegant aesthetic. Perhaps the most typical element is the cabriole leg, at first plain and finished with a simple turned pad foot, and later developing into a highly carved element complete with ball-and-claw, hairy-paw, or lion's foot. Furniture was made by cabinetmakers rather than joiners, and the list of American Chippendales is long (Thomas Chippendale was the most famous English cabinetmaker of the period and by whose name furniture of the middle of the period is often known). It includes the Goddards and Townsends of Newport, R.I., and many notable Philadelphia makers, including William Savery, Thomas Affleck, and Benjamin Randolph.

Side Chair, ca. 1780

- Typical Chippendale style
- Mahogany
- Square back
- Cupid-bow crest rail
- Pierced and carved splat
- Highly carved, squared-off cabriole front legs
- Ball-and-claw feet
- Stump rear legs
- Rectilinear seat

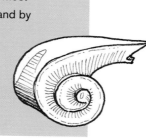

Arm terminal volute

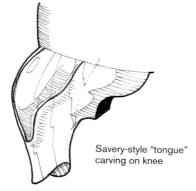

Savery-style "tongue" carving on knee

Kneehole Desk (Bureau), ca. 1765

- Made by John Townsend of Newport, R.I.
- Mahogany, with poplar as a secondary wood
- Block and shell front
- Shell-carved kneehole door
- Bracket feet
- Solid top
- Single, wide drawer
- Two tiers of narrow drawers
- Closely related to the highboy on the opposite page, this is essentially the lower half of a chest on chest with a kneehole cupboard

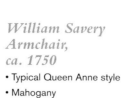

**William Savery
Armchair,
ca. 1750**

- Typical Queen Anne style
- Mahogany
- Rounded back
- Plain, profiled splat
- Not much carving, except for volutes and shells
- Cabriole front legs
- Simple trifid feet

Tea Table, ca. 1780

- Philadelphia-round type
- Mahogany
- "Pie-crust" scalloped edge
- Tilting top
- Fluted pillar
- Richly carved legs
- Tripod legs
- Ball-and-claw feet

Tea Table, ca. 1750

- New England-rectangular style
- Maple; originally painted red
- Markedly slender cabriole legs
- Pad feet
- Deeply scalloped apron

High Chest of Drawers (Highboy), ca. 1770

- High-style work typical of Philadelphia cabinetmakers
- Chest-on-chest, double-case construction
- Richly carved, broken scroll bonnet
- Carved corners
- Carved cabriole legs with ball-and-claw feet at front and back
- Sophisticated proportions, progressively graduated drawers
- Veneered casework

Federal Period, 1780-1840

After the Revolution, American tastes and sympathies transferred from Britain to France, especially with regard to furniture styles. The French Empire style planned and fostered by Napoleon was adopted and distinctively modified by American cabinetmakers and is typically known as Federal style. In comparison to the light and well-proportioned furniture typified by the Hepplewhite- and Sheraton-style pieces of the end of the Mahogany Period and the early days of the Federal Period, much Federal furniture is dark, heavy, and vulgar. The finest, however, is often superb and owes much to one of the most famous of all American cabinetmakers, Duncan Phyfe, a New York woodworker possessed of great taste and a wonderful eye for proportion.

Typical
Hepplewhite pull

Table, ca. 1810–1820

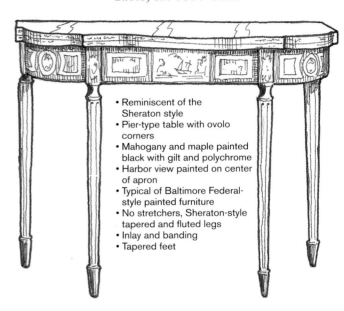

- Reminiscent of the Sheraton style
- Pier-type table with ovolo corners
- Mahogany and maple painted black with gilt and polychrome
- Harbor view painted on center of apron
- Typical of Baltimore Federal-style painted furniture
- No stretchers, Sheraton-style tapered and fluted legs
- Inlay and banding
- Tapered feet

Lyre-back Side Chair, ca. 1815

- Klismos-type chair with classical details, made by Duncan Phyfe
- Mahogany
- Shaggy front legs
- Hairy-paw feet
- Lyre splat
- Heavily reeded
- Graceful curves
- Light, stretcherless construction

Secretary, ca. 1820

- Highly varnished
- Veneered construction
- Massive in scale and proportion
- High-style Philadelphia Federal bureau, French Empire-inspired
- Mahogany and bird's-eye maple

The 19th Century, 1840-1910

The mid-19th century saw mass-production become the norm in all areas of American life—from farming to high-end furniture making. Some furniture historians refer to this as the era of the "degraded style," and while commercialism certainly resulted in a lot of cheap, shoddy and undistinguished work, there also was a remarkable burgeoning of vigorous new styles, some unabashedly derivative, including Rococo Revival, Egyptian Revival, Gothic Revival, and Italian Revival.

Nineteenth-century furniture (which is often referred to as Victorian—after the reigning British monarch) tends to be thought of as extremely ornamented, overstuffed, and often in terrible taste, but it also includes much innovative elegance, typified by pieces from makers such as Emile Gallé, Louis Majorelle, Michael Thonet, Charles Voysey, and Charles Eastlake. There is, in fact, no one common characteristic of the period other than that of diversity.

Library Table, ca. 1880

- Typical of the Modern Gothic style
- Ebonized cherry
- Inspired by the craft traditions of the Middle Ages
- Supposed honesty of construction and materials
- No applied ornamentation

Side Chair, ca. 1880

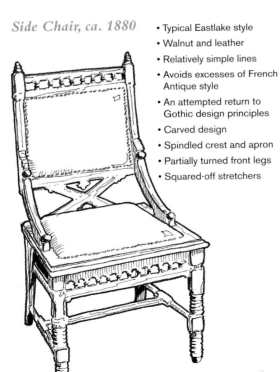

- Typical Eastlake style
- Walnut and leather
- Relatively simple lines
- Avoids excesses of French Antique style
- An attempted return to Gothic design principles
- Carved design
- Spindled crest and apron
- Partially turned front legs
- Squared-off stretchers

Cabinet, ca. 1876

- Classical motifs
- Elaborate marquetry panels
- Typical of Renaissance Revival style
- Carved, curved, and applied gilt ornamentation
- Maximum opulence
- Rosewood

Shaker, 1800-1900

Throughout the 19th century, the Shaker communities were producing furniture so different from everything else being made that the furniture is now recognized as a major American style. Its essential quality is simplicity. Eschewing ornamentation, the Shakers made furniture that not only was eminently practical and honest but also possessed a restrained elegance. Often giving the appearance of great delicacy, Shaker pieces are nonetheless constructed on sound and sturdy principles and have been the original inspiration for many a woodworker attracted by their straight lines and lack of ornamentation.

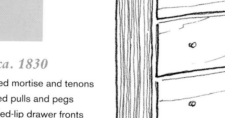

Cupboard-Chest, ca. 1830

- Pine; originally painted red
- Simplicity of form offset by sophisticated joinery
- Raised panels
- Pinned mortise and tenons
- Turned pulls and pegs
- Molded-lip drawer fronts
- Fully dovetailed drawers

Side Chair, ca. 1840

- Woven tape seat
- Seemingly simple, but thoughtfully designed and carefully constructed
- Slats graduated to become wider from bottom to top
- Tops of slats are beveled
- Back legs outfitted with "tilters" for greater comfort (tilters allow you to lean back in the chair without damaging it)

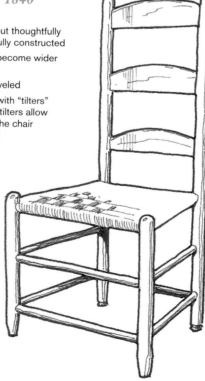

Side Table, ca. 1830

- The quintessential Shaker table
- Cherry, with pine interiors
- Tapered legs, turned at feet
- Large top with wide overhang
- No molding, carving, or inlay
- Fully dovetailed, flush-front drawer

Arts and Crafts, 1890-1920

Reacting against the fashionable excesses and often shoddy work of mass production, the English designer William Morris inspired a generation of American furniture designers dedicated to honesty, utility and, above all, good-quality workmanship. Charles and Henry Greene, Gustav Stickley, Ralph Whitehead (who founded the Byrdcliffe Arts Colony) and the anonymous craftsmen of the Roycroft Community in East Aurora, N.Y., produced a body of furniture variously known as Mission, Arts and Crafts, and Craftsman furniture, which has remained popular—and distinct in style—to the present, taking its place as a legitimate major American style.

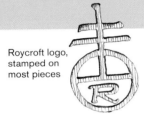

Roycroft logo, stamped on most pieces

Signature Roycroft bulbous foot on tapered leg

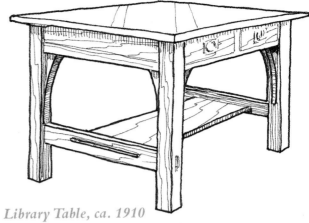

Library Table, ca. 1910

- Fumed white oak typical of Stickley furniture
- Rectilinear, with reverse flying-buttress corbels
- Exposed mortise-and-tenon joinery
- Structural integrity embodied by post-and-lintel design system
- Handwrought hardware

Dining Chair, ca. 1910

- White oak, leather seat
- Plain, Mission-style joinery with distinctive Roycroft tapered legs
- Bulbous feet
- Well-finished surfaces, with design emphasizing workmanship

Desk, ca. 1904

- Design by Greene and Greene
- Structural elements emphasized as design features
- White oak
- Protruding dowel ends
- Through-tenons
- Oversized battens
- Locking escutcheons
- Butterfly keys
- Proud partition edges

Quintessential Arts and Crafts

THE ARTS AND CRAFTS STYLE has been popular for a hundred years; there are examples in every antique and secondhand furniture store; reproductions abound; and it's a perennial favorite with woodworkers—but what exactly defines Arts and Crafts? Ask anyone familiar with the style—also known as Mission, Craftsman, Crafts, Cloister, or even Quaint—how they identify it, and you'll get answers that typically contain words such as "foursquare," "straightforward construction," "exposed joinery," and "quartersawn oak." Such elements make the Arts and Crafts style inviting to many woodworkers who are new to the craft and who are less intimidated by Arts and Crafts furniture than they are by other, more sophisticated styles. Despite its apparent simplicity, however, it's just as easy to get a piece of Arts and Crafts furniture wrong as it is to fail at your first attempt at constructing a Chippendale piece that features cabriole legs—unless you have a full understanding of what the essential design details are and how they work together.

It's true that the Arts and Crafts style originated partly in response to overdecorated and directionless 19th-century furniture, but equally important were concerns about the shoddy quality of mass-produced factory furniture and its effect not only on the consumer but also on the people who made it. Arts and Crafts was conceived as an essentially utilitarian style affordable by all; the idea that its manufacture should be something in which the maker could take pride was central to the philosophy underlying what became known as the Arts and Crafts movement.

A piece of furniture built in the genuine Arts and Crafts style is therefore first and foremost completely functional. The furniture is solidly constructed with a minimum of superfluous ornament, unashamed yet not boastful of its joinery and, more often than not, made of oak—which is a supremely appropriate wood for hardwearing furniture and a species that harks back to the period in furniture-making history when craftsmanship was valued more than commercial success.

The movement embodied the writings of a variety of influential 19th-century art critics, philosophers, architects, and designers such as John Ruskin and William Morris, as well as the work of 20th-century furniture makers Gustav Stickley (and his brothers), Elbert Hubbard, and the Roycrofters. Other seminal figures included the noted California architects Charles and Henry Greene, Frank Lloyd Wright, and

Influential Makers of the Era

By the late 1800s, the Industrial Revolution was changing the world of furniture: The individual craftsman was being supplanted by factory production as the leading influence on style. Driven strictly by commercial concerns, mechanization was overtaking what had been a craft with an aesthetic founded on tradition, training, and individual craftsmanship. The result was an abuse of style and an excess of indiscriminate decoration that took the form of a series of "revivals" produced primarily for the sake of novelty in an attempt to capture the market. The Arts and Crafts movement developed primarily in opposition to this trend, as designers, architects and furniture makers strove to produce items that placed a greater value on purer ideals of artistic honesty and craftsmanship. Initially, at least, the Arts and Crafts movement was more about what not to do than it was about a clearly defined new style. This is why there is such a broad range of pieces—spanning a long period—that can be identified as belonging to the Arts and Crafts style.

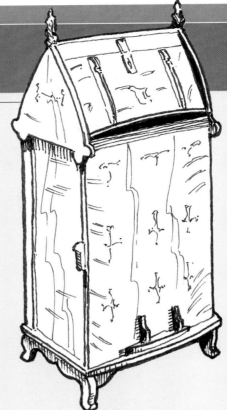

Charles Rohlfs
Drop-Front Desk, 1883

Heavily influenced by the Gothic style, Rohlfs was a leading figure in the American Arts and Crafts movement and was a friend of Elbert Hubbard (founder of the Roycroft Community at East Aurora, N.Y.). Rohlfs was influenced by modern designers such as Charles Rennie Macintosh and, as many other Arts and Crafts designers did, looked back to the Gothic Period in his use of oak, as exemplified by this desk.

Byrdcliffe Arts Colony
Wall Cabinet, 1904

This stained poplar cabinet, with a carved and polychromed door panel, was a typical product of the Byrdcliffe workshops in Woodstock, N.Y., founded by the wealthy Englishman Ralph Whitehead, who had been a student of the eminent Victorian art critic John Ruskin—the generally acknowledged father of the Arts and Crafts movement. Simplicity of design as well as individual craftsmanship in a communal environment inform this version of Arts and Crafts style.

Gustav Stickley
Armchair, 1902

Regarded by many as defining the style, Stickley's mass-produced pieces made of oak were the most commercially successful manifestation of Arts and Crafts furniture. Although his are among the most simple examples of the style, Stickley drew his inspiration from more sophisticated designers, such as Charles Voysey and William Lethaby in England.

internationally known and influential designers and furniture makers Charles Voysey, Ernest Gimson, and the Barnsley brothers.

Because the movement that resulted in this style of furniture began as far back as the middle of the 19th century, the range of design elements that belong to this style is, in fact, much broader than many people realize.

Six Quintessential Elements

Out of all the features that make Arts and Crafts furniture unique, there are six main elements that make this type of furniture noticeable and memorable.

1. Material Quartersawn oak does have much to recommend it: strength, durability, relative stability and an attractive figure characterized by the medullary rays not visible in flatsawn stock (see the top right drawing on the facing page). Although a hardwood, oak

is not excessively difficult to work—it is easier, in fact, to produce a crisp surface with a less than perfectly sharp tool on a piece of oak than on a piece of softwood. Oak is not toxic and may have a wide range of color— red, white, or brown—depending on the species. The wood also takes stain well and can be fumed, a technique that can produce a wonderful aged look. Although most factory-built Arts and Crafts furniture was made of oak, many well-known designers have used other species, such as walnut, mahogany, and cherry.

2. Construction techniques Although cabinet construction with veneered surfaces is occasionally used for the body of an Arts and Crafts piece, the majority of authentic pieces are made using solid wood and frame-and-panel construction.

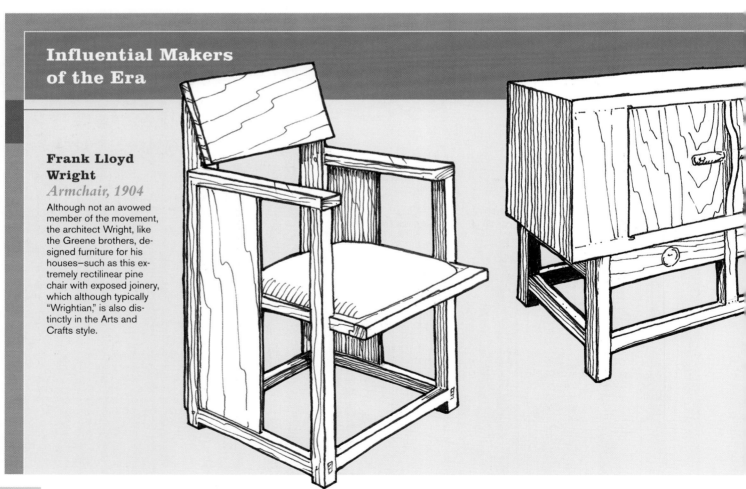

Influential Makers of the Era

Frank Lloyd Wright
Armchair, 1904

Although not an avowed member of the movement, the architect Wright, like the Greene brothers, designed furniture for his houses—such as this extremely rectilinear pine chair with exposed joinery, which although typically "Wrightian," is also distinctly in the Arts and Crafts style.

Consistent with the directness and honesty that are the hallmarks of this style is the use of slats where a solid piece or a frame-and-panel section would be overkill. Unlike the furniture of the Gothic Period, turned elements are rare in Arts and Crafts designs. All of this is in keeping with the principle of using the simplest possible methods of work for the most honest and unpretentious result.

Simple does not, however, mean sloppy, especially in terms of the construction of a piece. In fact, because the aim of the Arts and Crafts movement was to design furniture that the maker could be proud of, a nice execution, particularly of exposed joinery, is essential when building a genuine Arts and Crafts piece.

3. Joinery Without a doubt, the mortise and tenon is the king of Arts and Crafts joints (see the sidebar 4 on p. 18). Dovetailing,

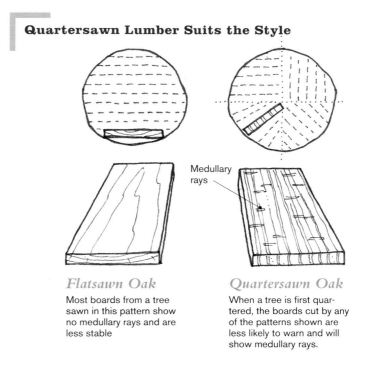

Quartersawn Lumber Suits the Style

Medullary rays

Flatsawn Oak
Most boards from a tree sawn in this pattern show no medullary rays and are less stable

Quartersawn Oak
When a tree is first quartered, the boards cut by any of the patterns shown are less likely to warn and will show medullary rays.

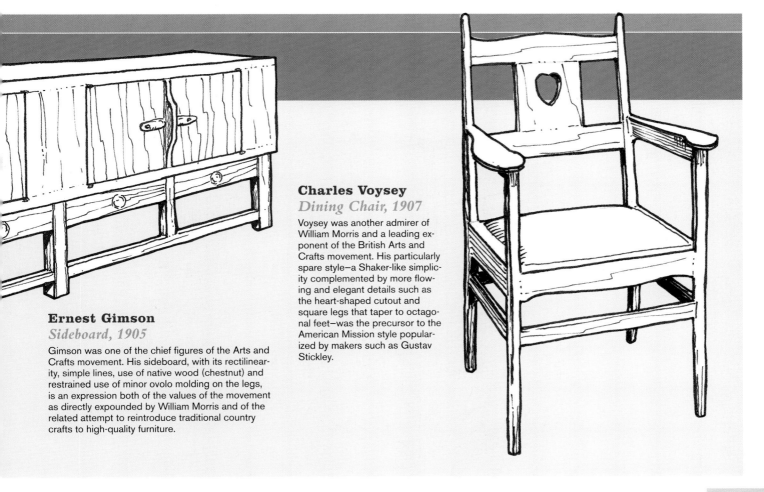

Ernest Gimson
Sideboard, 1905
Gimson was one of the chief figures of the Arts and Crafts movement. His sideboard, with its rectilinearity, simple lines, use of native wood (chestnut) and restrained use of minor ovolo molding on the legs, is an expression both of the values of the movement as directly expounded by William Morris and of the related attempt to reintroduce traditional country crafts to high-quality furniture.

Charles Voysey
Dining Chair, 1907
Voysey was another admirer of William Morris and a leading exponent of the British Arts and Crafts movement. His particularly spare style—a Shaker-like simplicity complemented by more flowing and elegant details such as the heart-shaped cutout and square legs that taper to octagonal feet—was the precursor to the American Mission style popularized by makers such as Gustav Stickley.

Paneling

Eighteenth- and nineteenth-century paneling typically has a frame consisting of stiles and rails of different widths, invariably molded on the inner edges surrounding a fielded or raised panel. Arts and Crafts paneling is typically square, with equal-width rails and stiles. Panels are sometimes carved, but more often than not they are plain and flat in unmolded frames.

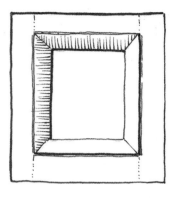 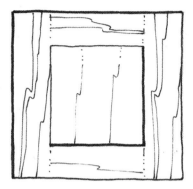

doweling, lapped, and housed joinery also are used where appropriate, but in keeping with the demands of strength and honesty, the mortise-and-tenon joint plays a major role in the majority of Arts and Crafts pieces.

Several varieties of tenons are used, including stub, blind, through-, and tusk, but each is used only when and where necessary for maximum strength without compromise. This means that if, for example, a through-tenon is the strongest possible form in a given situation, the design will make a virtue of the necessity by not attempting to hide or disguise the joint. This results in the ends of through-tenons being finished a little proud of the surface, often nicely chamfered and with any wedges

Influential Makers of the Era

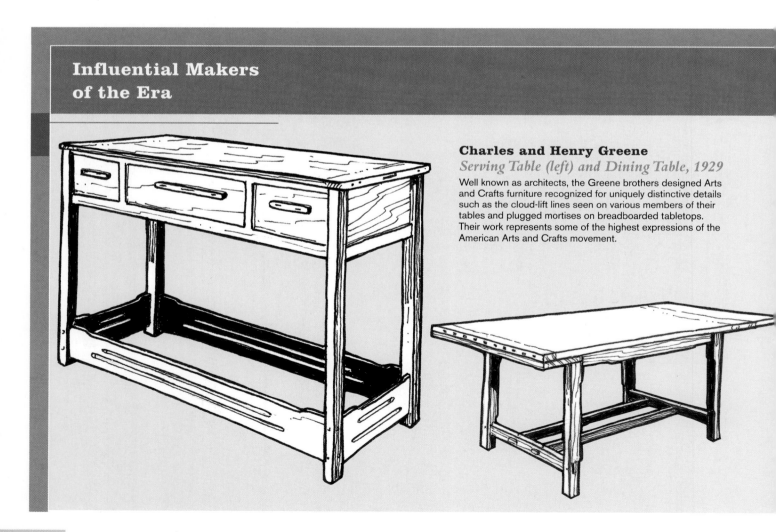

Charles and Henry Greene
Serving Table (left) and Dining Table, 1929

Well known as architects, the Greene brothers designed Arts and Crafts furniture recognized for uniquely distinctive details such as the cloud-lift lines seen on various members of their tables and plugged mortises on breadboarded tabletops. Their work represents some of the highest expressions of the American Arts and Crafts movement.

thoughtfully arranged for a pleasing visual pattern and the most efficient use.

4. Design paradigms In American Arts and Crafts pieces, whether of the mass-produced variety typified by Gustav Stickley's Craftsman furniture or the higher-end custom designs of the Greene brothers, there is an immediate impression of squareness. This is most evident in the profiles of tops, edges, and other flat surfaces, such as broad chair arms. Molding is almost completely absent, sharp edges are gently relieved but not rounded, and overhangs are kept to a minimum.

Although many details are, in fact, square—such as in paneled framing, where a bottom rail wider than other frame members is rare (see the drawing on the facing page), and in the design of glazed doors, where all panes are equally square—absolute squareness is largely illusory, and slopes and curves are common. It is not that the style is inelegant—many pieces can be found based on elegant design paradigms such as the golden rectangle (see the drawing on p. 18)—but the strength and utility of a piece always dominate.

Both gently and boldly formed curves are common in skirts, chair rails, and the lower edges of cabinet sides, but they are invariably simple and rarely compound, except for occasional tight cutouts on stool bases. Such shapes, including ogees and intersecting arcs, are nods to the influence of medieval Gothic oak furniture, much valued by leaders of the Arts and Crafts style

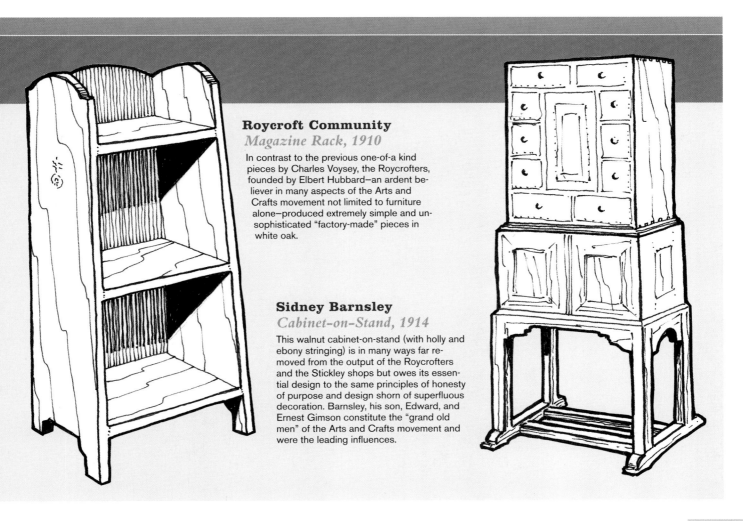

Roycroft Community
Magazine Rack, 1910

In contrast to the previous one-of-a-kind pieces by Charles Voysey, the Roycrofters, founded by Elbert Hubbard—an ardent believer in many aspects of the Arts and Crafts movement not limited to furniture alone—produced extremely simple and unsophisticated "factory-made" pieces in white oak.

Sidney Barnsley
Cabinet-on-Stand, 1914

This walnut cabinet-on-stand (with holly and ebony stringing) is in many ways far removed from the output of the Roycrofters and the Stickley shops but owes its essential design to the same principles of honesty of purpose and design shorn of superfluous decoration. Barnsley, his son, Edward, and Ernest Gimson constitute the "grand old men" of the Arts and Crafts movement and were the leading influences.

Designing Using the Golden Rectangle

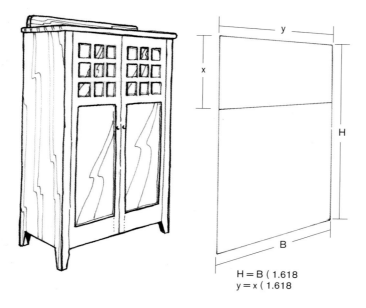

$$H = B \, (1.618$$
$$y = x \, (1.618$$

The perfect squareness of the upper glazing and the general rectilinearity of this cabinet are based on a sophisticated design paradigm in which the height (H) equals the base (B) multiplied by 1.618, a proportion called the golden rectangle. The upper portion of the cabinet also is a golden rectangle.

for its craftsmanship and honesty. Curved yet square-edged brackets are another common feature of many pieces.

One other detail that would seem to belie an apparent squareness and angularity is the frequent use of tapered legs. The tapers, however, are usually limited to a short section near the base. Tapering legs like this prevents the piece from appearing too heavy, but because the tapers are equally formed on all four sides of the leg, a general feeling of squareness persists.

5. Decoration Despite a superficial plainness characterized by square edges, the lack of molding, the use of a relatively homogenous material, and the flatness of panels, Arts and Crafts furniture often is decorated with a variety of techniques ranging from simple curved cutouts to delicate floral inlays (see the sidebar on the facing page). Reflecting a continuing sensitivity to other styles and fashions on the part of designers such as Harvey Ellis or Charles Rennie Macintosh, who are perhaps better known for their Art

Mortise-and-Tenon Joinery

Stronger and more appropriate than dowels or biscuits, mortise-and-tenon joints may be unshouldered (as for seatback slats) or shouldered on anywhere from one to four sides, depending on their intended use and particular design.

Decorative Reinforcements

Lacking applied ornamentation, the exposed joinery of Arts and Crafts furniture became the primary decorative element.

Pinned Mortise and Tenon

Tusk Mortise and Tenon

Blind Mortise and Tenon

Two shoulders (seat rails)

Four shoulders (stretchers)

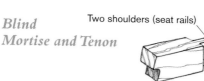

Wedged Mortise and Tenon

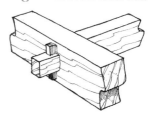

Brackets and Cutouts

Not all details are perfectly rectilinear. Small accents, many in the form of brackets or cutouts, enliven otherwise straightforward designs.

The angularity of wedges and curved cutouts lends a refined look to Arts and Crafts pieces.

Brackets, though square-edged, unmolded and flat, often are given a gently curved profile.

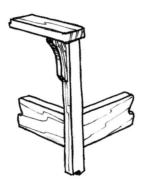 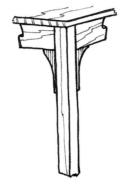 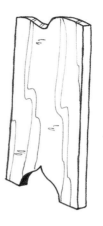 

Nouveau styles, the influence of the more flowing, nature-based Art Nouveau style is felt in many Arts and Crafts pieces—for example, in the products of various "utopian" workshops such as the Byrdcliffe Arts Colony in Woodstock, N.Y.—in the form of pastel-colored painted sections, tulip inlays, and lily patterns.

Central to the principle of craftsmanship in this style of furniture is the use of other natural materials, such as reed and rush for seats, leather upholstery, and hand-wrought hardware made from iron or hammered brass. The hardware often is as square and sturdy as the furniture it serves and stands in complete contrast to the elegant and finely wrought shapes found on 18th-century pieces or the overworked fantastic shapes common on much 19th-century furniture. A gratuitous form of decoration in terms of structural function, but one that is consistent with the incorporation of natural materials, is the frequent use of a row of hand-wrought nails as an edge decoration.

6. Finish It would be inappropriate to finish an Arts and Crafts piece with a glossy lacquer. But while natural finishes like simple oiling and waxing may predominate, other processes, such as filling, staining, and fuming, are common.

Careful surface preparation is most important. In the case of an open-grained wood like oak, a matching wood filler should be used. If oak is filled first, it then may be waxed or perhaps lightly oiled and then waxed. If wax alone is used, it should be colored so that the wax-filled pores in the wood do not show white.

Fuming, the process of exposing oak to the fumes of ammonia, is a common method of turning oak darker without producing the irregular color that can result from careless staining. The popularity of fuming, especially among early proponents of Arts and Crafts furniture, resulted from the misconception that genuine Gothic furniture was extremely dark. That darkness, in fact, came from centuries of exposure to smoky atmospheres. When new, however, most Gothic furniture was brightly painted or valued precisely for its light golden color.

GRAHAM BLACKBURN is a furniture maker, author, illustrator and the publisher of Blackburn Books (www.blackburnbooks.com).

Building in the Language of Greene and Greene

BY THOMAS HUGH
STANGELAND

I MADE A ROOMFUL OF FURNITURE recently in the style of Charles and Henry Greene, brothers who designed houses and furniture in California in the first decades of this century. One of the most difficult aspects of making this furniture was finding ways to produce the details, the little touches that define the Greenes' work and make it so appealing to the hand and eye. The square black pegs, which are left slightly proud of the mahogany surface; the exposed splines also proud and gently radiused back to the surrounding wood; the rounded double-L brackets—these and other signatures of the Greenes' furniture are all deceptively tricky to make well. Once mastered, though, they provide the basic vocabulary for building furniture in the language of Greene and Greene.

The dining chair in the photo on p. 22, one of a set of eight I built, is a straight reproduction of a chair designed by the Greenes in 1908. Working from photographs, I followed their example as closely as I could. The only concession the client and I made to cost was to leave out a subtle carving detail at the base of the legs. I took a more interpretive approach when I made the sideboard in the photo on the facing page and the writing table in the inset photo at left. For each of these, I used a Greene and Greene piece as a starting point but redesigned the original to satisfy the client's needs, the demands of function, and my own sense of proportion. (For an account of how the sideboard evolved from its Greene and Greene forefather to my final version, see the sidebar on pp. 26–27.)

Springs of Inspiration

The Greenes' system of detailing did not develop all at once. It grew gradually as they were exposed to a variety of influences and ideas. Like many craftsmen of their day, Greene and Greene were deeply influenced by the Arts-and-Crafts movement. Arising in 19th-century England in reaction to the mechanization and shoddy goods of the industrial revolution, the movement was a call for honest hand craftsmanship. The Greenes were particularly influenced by Gustav Stickley and other proponents of Arts and Crafts who emphasized openly expressed joinery and function before frippery—features also evident in all the Greenes' work.

What sets the Greenes' work apart is the blending of an Oriental aesthetic with Arts and Crafts. In Japanese temple architecture and Chinese furniture, the Greenes saw ways to soften a composition of straight lines and solids by rounding edges and introducing

gentle curves. There's an Eastern overtone as well in the balanced but slightly asymmetrical patterns of the Greenes' detailing.

Attention to Detail Includes the Material

The impact of the details in the Greenes' furniture is partly a function of the materials they used. Combining ebony and mahogany gives the furniture warmth as well as a strong visual contrast. I wanted to achieve the same effects but without using endangered woods. I considered using maple with walnut accents, but I finally chose sustained-yield mahogany and Ebon-X™, an ebony substitute made of chemically altered walnut. The chemical treatment gives the Ebon-X a rich black color but also gives it working properties that aren't that far from ebony's.

Square pegs Glinting, square ebony pegs are a hallmark of Greene and Greene furniture. The pegs rise above the mahogany, and each little edge is gently radiused back to the surrounding wood, providing a reflective surface and a tactile message of hand craftsmanship. The pegs emphasize the joints in the furniture and many are caps for counterbored screws. But as I laid out the mortises for them on the crest rails of the chairs, I realized that some of the pegs are purely decorative. I followed the Greenes' example in making the pegs in a variety of sizes, from ³⁄₁₆ to ½ in. sq. As far as I could tell, the variation in size was a matter of aesthetics. I found, too, that their placement was not exactly symmetrical. Rather than being lined up in rows, the pegs were arranged in subsets slightly offset from each other to add visual interest (see the top right photo on p. 22).

SWEET DETAILS **define the furniture of Greene and Greene. Learning to produce them is key to making furniture that compares to the originals. The author's sideboard (above) and writing desk (facing page) are fresh designs, but their superbly made and marshalled details give them the ring of the real thing. Both are made of sustained-yield mahogany and Ebon-X, an ebony substitute.**

REPRODUCING DETAILS—**Square black pegs left proud convey the Greenes' message of hand craftsmanship in the author's reproduction chair.**

be the exposed surface of the pegs: achieving a totally smooth surface was essential.

It would be murder to make the tiny radiused edges with the pegs already in their mortises, so I did my shaping ahead of time. I rounded down slightly on each edge at the end of the stick with an orbital sander, keeping the roundovers equal. To get the gleam of polished ebony, I took the sticks to my grinder and burnished the ends with red rouge on a cotton buff wheel.

When I was satisfied with the finish, I bandsawed about ⅜ in. off each end of all the sticks and repeated the process until I had a good supply of pegs. The bandsawn face would be hidden in the mortise, so I didn't have to clean it up. But I did chamfer the four bottom edges, so they wouldn't hang up or cause tearout when I drove the peg into the mortise. I did the chamfering on my stationary belt sander, holding the little pegs by hand (leave your fingernails a little long for this chore). Or you could do the chamfering against a stationary piece of sandpaper on a flat surface. I put a little glue in the mortise and drove the pegs with a rubber mallet.

I made ¼-in.-deep mortises for the dozens of pegs with my hollow-chisel mortiser. It makes the job quick; the little tearout is not noticeable after I drive in the slightly oversized pegs. You could also use a drill and chisels or chop the mortises by hand.

To make the pegs, I ripped 8- or 10-in.-long sticks of Ebon-X, so they were exactly square in section and fractionally larger than the corresponding mortises. I squared up both ends of each stick on the disc sander with the stick held against the miter gauge. I sanded out the disc scratches with 150-grit paper on my hand-held orbital sander. These sanded ends would eventually

BRACKET ALIGNMENT IS TRICKY–The author locates a dowel hole on his table by sliding the bracket along a guide board clamped to the apron and marking with a dowel center.

Curved brackets

Those little double-L brackets below the seat of the chair and the cases of the sideboard and writing table are derived from Chinese furniture. In addition to tying parts together visually and adding a curve, they provide some resistance to racking forces (see the top photo). While they may look innocent, they're quite a challenge to make.

I made the brackets in bunches. I made a Masonite® template for each size L and traced it over and over on a board machined to the correct width and thickness. Because the wide end of the L would be face glued, I put it on the edge of the board to give it a long grain surface. I cut the brackets out on the bandsaw and then sanded their outside curves on my stationary disc sander and their inside curves with a sanding drum chucked into my drill press. To be sure I had flat, square glue surfaces, I touched them up using the miter gauge with my stationary disc sander.

All the curved edges on the fronts of the brackets are rounded over, and I did the work with a router inverted in a vise. If you make a small push block with a foam or rubber bottom surface, you'll be able to get your hands away from the action while

**Fig. 1:
Bracket Joinery**

Face-glued joint

Rail

Face-glued joint

Leg

Dowel joints

Bracket

*What sets the Greenes'
work apart is the blending
of an Oriental aesthetic
with Arts and Crafts.*

keeping good pressure on the little workpiece. Because the grain changed direction as I routed around the bend, I found it was important to go fairly quickly and maintain even pressure.

I doweled pairs of L's together and then doweled and face-glued them to the furniture, as shown in Figure 1. To drill the dowel holes in the L's, I clamped them in my drill-press vise with stop blocks set up to keep them oriented properly as I tightened the vise.

Gluing up the brackets was a two-stage operation. First I joined the two L's. I laid them on the tablesaw (any reliably flat surface will do) and pushed the dowel joint together by hand. I found if I held them for 30 to 40 seconds, I could leave them and they'd stay tight. When they were dry, I gave them a quick hit on the belt sander to make sure the glue surfaces were flat and square.

The second stage was gluing the brackets in place. To locate the dowel hole in the leg, I put a dowel center in the bracket and slid the bracket along a guide board to

mark the spot (see the inset photo on p. 23). After I'd drilled the dowel hole, I clamped the bracket in place using one small quick-release clamp to pull the dowel joint tight and another to keep pressure on the face joint.

Exposed splines The arms on the chairs I made are joined to the front legs with large splines shaped in a shallow S. Like the square pegs, the splines are left proud of the surrounding wood and gently radiused back to meet it. The sinuous black line of the Ebon-X in the mahogany arm emphasizes the joint and underscores its double curve. Here the spline is structural, but where a similar element appears in the breadboard ends of the sideboard and writing table, it is purely decorative.

I made the loose splines for the chair by temporarily screwing a rough-cut dummy spline in the joint and flush-trimming it to the shape of the arm with a router. I removed it and used it as a template with a straight router bit and an oversized bearing wheel to turn out Ebon-X splines ⅛ in. proud of the arm. As with the pegs, I did

EXPOSED SPLINES MASKED MOVEMENT of solid panels in the Greene's work. But the plywood top (right) won't move. So the spline (facing page) is glued to both the panel and breadboard end.

PULLS CAN MAKE OR BREAK a piece of furniture: Experiment to find the right one by mocking up a range of pulls.

the sanding, radiusing, and burnishing on the exposed edges of the splines before screwing and gluing them in place.

Breadboard on the sideboard I made the tops of my sideboard and desk breadboard style, as the Greenes did. The breadboard ends are decorative in my piece because I used a veneered plywood panel and didn't have to accommodate seasonal movement. The ends are solid mahogany, biscuited and glued to the panel. At the front, I inserted false loose splines of Ebon-X. Because the breadboard ends extend beyond the panel, the splines had to follow in a shallow S-shape, as shown in Figure 2.

I routed mortises for the splines with a slot-cutter fitted with a bearing wheel. After chiseling out the ends of the mortises, I cut Ebon-X splines to length and rough-cut their back edges to the shallow S-shape on the bandsaw. Like the square pegs, the false splines stand proud of the surface, so I put them in temporarily and scribed a line following the contour on the edge but spaced away 1/8 in. Then I removed the splines, and bandsawed to the line. I gently radiused the edges that would be exposed, sanded and burnished them and glued them in place.

Pulls If a door or a drawer front could be compared to clothing on a person, then knobs and pulls would be like neckties, pins, and earrings—finishing touches that are key to the overall impact of a piece. I used the same type of pull on the table drawers as I made for the sideboard. I tried a number of different sizes before settling on the right one for each piece, as shown in the inset photo on the facing page. The pulls are a variation on the Asian "cloud lift," an abstract representation of clouds found throughout the Greenes' work. I bandsawed the pulls and filed and sanded to finished shape; then I radiused the edges with a router. I had to scale them down

considerably from the ones used on the sideboard. For the sideboard, I decorated them with square pegs, but on the smaller pulls for the writing desk, I found they looked cramped so I left them off.

A fitting finish I wanted the pieces I made to have an immediate presence, a feeling of having been around for a long time: In a sense, they had been. To achieve it, I treated the wood with potassium dichromate, an oxidizing agent borrowed from photographic processing. It comes in powder form and is mixed with water and sponged on. Before applying it, I wet-sanded every surface to raise the grain and knock it back down. While applying the potassium dichromate, I kept an air hose handy to disperse the puddles that formed in the inside corners. If they are left to stand and soak in, the color will be uneven. I then sprayed three coats of catalyzed lacquer, sanding between coats with 320-grit paper.

THOMAS HUGH STANGELAND is a professional furniture maker in Seattle, Wash.

Fig. 1: Exposed Spline for Breadboard Ends

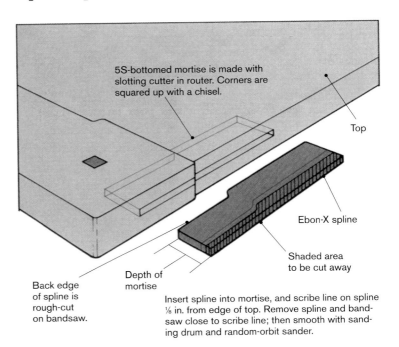

5S-bottomed mortise is made with slotting cutter in router. Corners are squared up with a chisel.

Top

Ebon-X spline

Shaded area to be cut away

Depth of mortise

Back edge of spline is rough-cut on bandsaw.

Insert spline into mortise, and scribe line on spline 1/8 in. from edge of top. Remove spline and bandsaw close to scribe line; then smooth with sanding drum and random-orbit sander.

A New Greene and Greene Sideboard

With my reproduction Greene and Greene chairs around his dining table, my client asked if I would make a sideboard to go with them. I quickly agreed but soon found it to be an entirely different undertaking. Reproducing the chairs had been a matter of mechanics: I had to figure out how to do what the Greenes had done. But making something in their style to fit a specific site would be a matter of interpretation.

My starting point for the commission was a sideboard the Greenes made in 1909. But I would have had to contort the original to make it fit the site. The three drawings on the facing page show the development of my sideboard: the Greene's original (top), a drawing midway in the adaptation (center) and the final version (bottom).

SITE SPECIFICS

The client intended the sideboard to be a visual anchor at the end of the room, so it had to be visible above the backs of the dining chairs. And it had to fill a long alcove. These requirements brought the sideboard's overall dimensions to 7 ft. long and 42 in. high—quite a bit longer and higher than a typical sideboard. I would have to do all I could to keep the piece from looking abnormally high.

REAPPORTIONMENT

The Greenes' sideboard has doors at each end and a bank of wide drawers in between. I decided to change this arrangement for several reasons. First, because the sideboard had to be so long, drawers located in the center would wind up being far larger from side to side than they were from front to back: a recipe for drawers that bind. I also thought wide, central drawers would emphasize the length of the piece. And my client, who entertains on a large scale, was concerned that the cabinets in the original were on the small side. I solved all these problems by moving the doors together into the middle, so they would open on one large cabinet and by

splitting the drawers into two banks, one on either side of the doors, as shown in the center drawing.

To help mask the height of the sideboard, I resorted to unusual proportioning on the drawers. Where a normal silverware drawer is 3 in. high, I made these 6 in. It would have been possible to stay closer to normal sizes if I had added a fourth drawer, but having more drawers in a stack emphasizes the vertical lines. I also preferred the appearance of three drawers. Call it mystic balance if you will, but an odd number of drawers always looks better to me.

HOW MANY LEGS?

The Greenes' sideboard has eight legs joined by wide stretchers. I decided to omit the stretchers and adopted the bracket detail from the chair to add decoration and a bit more strength below the case. But the number of legs didn't seem right. I did a sketch of a sideboard with four legs, but I thought such a long sideboard would appear ill-supported on four legs even if it could have been made soundly. I drew a version with eight legs (see the center drawing). But that tended to emphasize the height of the piece and made for a clutter of brackets. So I drew a version with six legs; that immediately looked right to me.

PLATE RAIL

With the placement of the legs, doors, and drawers determined, I turned to the plate rail. The Greenes' sideboard has a low, solid plate rail. I wanted something that would lighten the sideboard and relate to the brackets, so I designed a low, open plate rail by adapting the bracket shape, stretching it out horizontally. I also took the opportunity to make a visual link to the legs. By creating a vertical center point in the plate rail, I carried through the line of the middle leg.

I used my bracket-making techniques to produce the parts of the plate rail. I doweled the parts together as before, but because the assembled rail was somewhat delicate, I screwed it to the sideboard's top from below rather than gluing it. This way, I could transport it separately and then attach it on site.

Evolution of a Sideboard

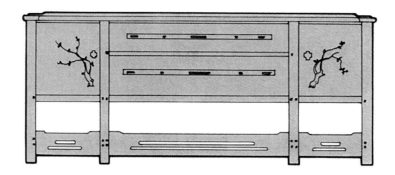

Sketch for Thorsen House sideboard, Greene and Greene, 1909

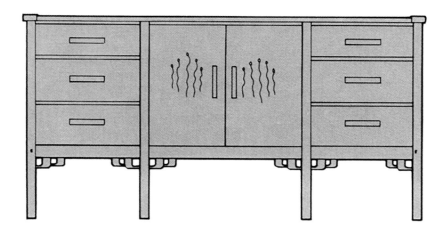

Early sketch for the author's sideboard

Doors have been moved to the middle to make the cabinet more spacious. The wide stretchers have been removed in favor of brackets.

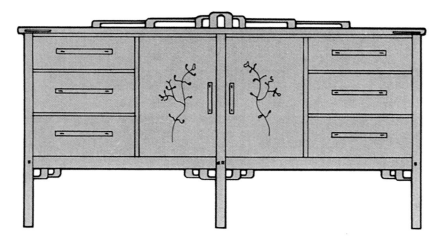

Final version of the sideboard

Two legs have been eliminated, giving the piece a more horizontal appearance. Bracket form has been adapted to make an open plate rail. Drawer handles have been elongated. The stylized tulip inlay of the earlier version, drawn from the chair splats, has been replaced with a more naturalistic composition.

Elements of the Shaker Style

BY CHRISTIAN
BECKSVOORT

WOODWORKING MASTERS Jere Osgood, Sam Maloof and George Nakashima each evolved a style and explored it to its ultimate conclusion, and to hell with what was in vogue. The Shakers did the same thing, continually refining their idiom until they approached perfection, without regard to the latest trend. They developed a style of furniture that blends well and fits comfortably in any type of house. The Shakers went out of their way to eschew fashion: The result is timelessness.

I grew up in a house full of Danish modern furniture, which was, it turns out, heavily influenced by Shaker designs. Like the Danish furniture makers, I fell under the sway of Shaker furniture the moment I discovered it—in my case, during a slide lecture in an architecture appreciation course I took in college. The simplicity and utility of the furniture I saw in the slides stunned me. In the late 1970s, I began restoring Shaker furniture, and much of my own work has been in the Shaker vein ever since. I very seldom reproduce slavishly, but you can look at my work and without batting an eye see its derivation is Shaker.

To make a Shaker-looking piece, adopt a Shaker attitude: Keep it simple in design and materials, make it functional, and in-corporate authentic details. The details shown on these pages were commonly used by the Shakers until about 1860, after which their furniture began to show the worldly influence of the Victorian style.

The Shakers believed "that which has in itself the highest use possesses the greatest beauty." It took the rest of the world nearly a century to come to the same conclusion, when, in the early 20th century, Louis Sullivan declared "form follows function." But these dictums alone do not lead inevitably to a particular style, much less to a specific set of elements and details. In addition to being inspired by their beliefs, the Shakers and the furniture they made were influenced by their historical context.

In short, the Shakers took the furniture they were familiar with, the local styles from New England to Kentucky, and stripped it of superfluous ornamentation. The Shaker craftsman Orren Haskins (1815-1892) perhaps said it best: "Why patronize the outside world? . . . We want a good plain substantial Shaker article, yea, one that bears credit to our profession and tells who and what we are, true and honest before the world, without hypocrisy or any false covering. The world at large can scarcely keep pace with itself in its stiles and fassions which last but a short time, when

CHERRY CUPBOARD 80 IN. BY 44 IN. BY 19 IN. **Canterbury, N.H., Circa 1850-1900**

Crown Moldings

Moldings along the tops of Shaker case pieces are hard to justify as anything but decorative. Most styles of furniture (and architecture) incorporate moldings or some type of overhang at the top. To the eye, a crown molding or overhang denotes an ending; it is much like a period at the end of a sentence. The Shakers, presumably, were not immune to this near-universal need for closure.

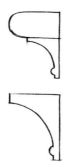

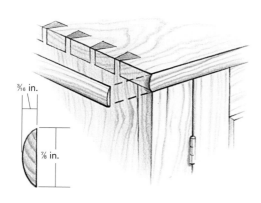

¾₆ in.

⅞ in.

Base Moldings

Shaker craftsmen used base moldings and profiled bracket bases for protection, not decoration. A rounded or shaped edge is far less prone to splintering or chipping than is a sharp, square corner. This is especially true near the floor, where base molds and brackets are likely to encounter brooms and mops or shoes and boots.

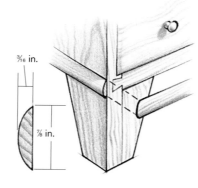

¾₆ in.

⅞ in.

something still more worthless or absurd takes its place. Let good enough alone, and take good common sense for our guide in all our pursuits, and we are safe within and without."

Shaker furniture, especially from the classic period of 1820 to 1850, contains little in the way of excessive moldings and virtually no carving or veneer. The Shakers favored native materials and were dead set against materials they felt were decadent, such as brass. The Western communities tended to follow the local vernacular style to a much greater degree than their Eastern counterparts. So the Shaker furniture from Ohio and Kentucky appears more ornate.

Some forms of furniture were never built by the Shakers. You will never see Shaker coffee tables, for example, nor tea tables, highboys, pencil-post beds or upholstered pieces. Some furniture companies market these items "in the Shaker style," including improbable pieces such as entertainment centers.

Certain elements appear over and over in Shaker furniture and make sense within the idiom. In striving for a design that remains faithful to the Shaker style, be mindful of their approach—just as you wouldn't build Queen Anne out of poplar, you wouldn't build Shaker out of rosewood. And pay close attention to the details.

CHRISTIAN BECKSVOORT is the author of *The Shaker Legacy*, published by The Taunton Press.

Door Frames and Panels

The doors on early Shaker pieces usually had raised, fielded panels. Over time, however, the raised panel fell out of favor, perhaps because it appeared too decorative or possibly because the shoulder was seen as just another dust collector. In any event, the flat panel ultimately replaced the more traditional raised panel as the first choice of Shaker cabinetmakers. In the transition, the pillow panel, as I call it, was sometimes used. Instead of having a well-defined, shouldered field, the panel was planed on all four edges to fit the groove in the frame. The result was a field that was barely noticeable.

Although square-shouldered door frames were used on occasion, more often than not, the frames featured a quarter-round thumbnail profile along their inside edges. To me, this represents a perfect example of a utilitarian, as opposed to a strictly decorative, molding. Rounded edges along the inside of the door frame are much easier to keep clean than straight, square shoulders.

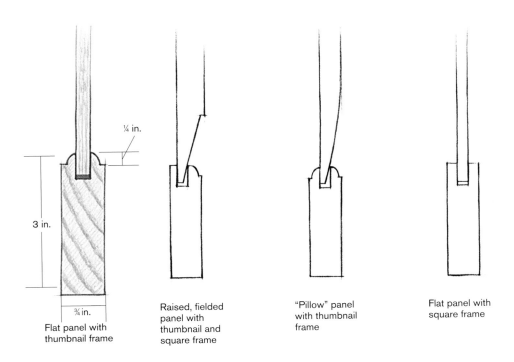

¼ in.

3 in.

¾ in.

Flat panel with thumbnail frame

Raised, fielded panel with thumbnail and square frame

"Pillow" panel with thumbnail frame

Flat panel with square frame

Drawers

Shaker craftsmen built both flush and lipped drawers. Flush drawers had square edges and fit fully into their openings. Lipped drawers, although more difficult to make, covered the gap around the drawer front to keep out dust. The lips, however, were usually on the top and two sides only. A lip on the bottom was considered too fragile, should the drawer have to be set on the ground. The quarter-round and thumbnail profiles were commonly used on all four edges of lipped drawers. Neither the Shakers nor their worldly contemporaries used the bevel-edged, raised door panel as a drawer front. That design fiasco was perpetrated on consumers by the kitchen-cabinet industry.

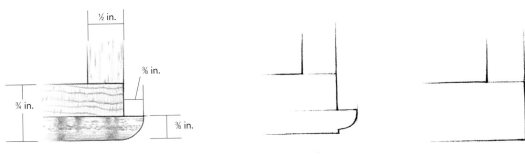

½ in.

⅜ in.

¾ in.

⅜ in.

Quarter-round, lipped

Thumbnail, lipped

Flush

Knobs

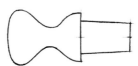

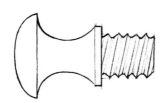

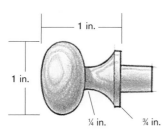

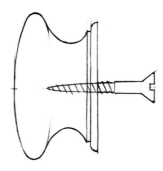

Shaker craftsmen continued the theme of simplicity right down to the knobs. Prior to the 1850s, most Shaker knobs were shopmade, although some early pieces had commercially manufactured porcelain knobs in either white or agate, a marbled brown color. After 1860, manufactured knobs became more and more common.

The typical Shaker knob was a variation of the mushroom form. Sizes ranged from ⅜ in. dia. on tiny desk drawers to 2¼ in. dia. on large built-ins. Knobs up to 1½ in. dia. were typically spindle turned, with either a plain tenon (glued and wedged through the door or drawer front) or a threaded tenon. Larger knobs were usually face turned and attached with steel screws from the inside. Shop-built Shaker knobs were always made of hardwoods, often of a contrasting species to the rest of the piece.

CHERRY SINGLE DROP-LEAF DESK
Top: 14½ in. by 30 in.
Leaf: 12 in.
Carcase: 12¾ in. by 20½ in.
Canterbury, N.H., Circa 1850-1900

Tabletop Edges

A fair number of Shaker tabletop edges were square or only slightly eased. A square edge, however, was by no means the only profile used. Shaker craftsmen realized that a simple, shaped profile was not only less prone to damage than a square edge but also less painful when bumped.

Rule joints were used on drop-leaf tables. The joint looked crisp and was less likely to lodge crumbs or pinch items hanging over the edges.

⅝ in.

Round

Eased edge   Ovolo   Bull nose   Chamfer   Double Chamfer

Legs and Turnings

Shaker table legs were, for the most part, quite simple. The double-tapered square leg was by far the most common form. The tapers were cut only on the two inside faces to give the leg a wider, sturdier stance and appearance. Another favorite leg was the straight-turned taper, most often seen on drop-leaf tables. These legs are often splayed a few degrees, because turned tapered legs attached at 90° to the top appear pigeon-toed. Swell tapers were

also popular. This form started a bit narrow under the shoulder, then swelled to a maximum diameter at one-quarter to one-half of the way down.

Shaker craftsmen handled the transition from the square area at the top of the leg to the turned portion in several ways. Frequently, they cut the shoulder perfectly square, a 90° cut with a parting tool. An easier, more common transition was the 45° cut, resulting in a rounded shoulder.

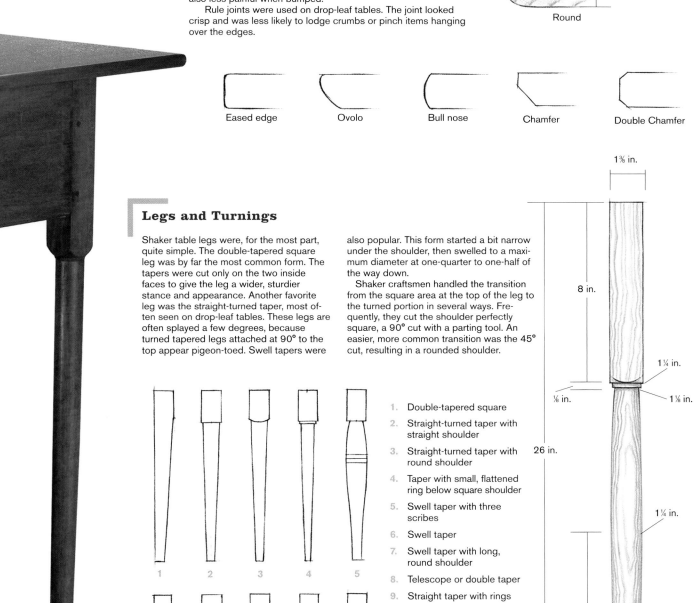

1. Double-tapered square
2. Straight-turned taper with straight shoulder
3. Straight-turned taper with round shoulder
4. Taper with small, flattened ring below square shoulder
5. Swell taper with three scribes
6. Swell taper
7. Swell taper with long, round shoulder
8. Telescope or double taper
9. Straight taper with rings
10. Swell taper with rings and pear foot

1⅜ in.

8 in.

1¼ in.

⅛ in.

1⅛ in.

26 in.

1¼ in.

12 in.

1 in.

Furniture Design: The Four Objectives

BY MIKE DUNBAR

WHEN YOU DESIGN a piece of furniture, you have four primary objectives. You may not be consciously aware of them, but they are part of your decision-making process.

The four goals are function, comfort, durability, and beauty. Although these are all very fundamental to woodworking, they deserve to be explored from time to time.

Does It Work?

For me the function of a piece is axiomatic. It must do its intended job. If the piece is a chair, it has to hold your backside off the ground. If it's a table, you must be able to sit at it, and you must be able to lie in a bed. Function implies a generally accepted definition of purpose.

A lot of ink has been spilled in the art-furniture debate—for example, is a chair that you can't sit in truly a chair? For most of us, who accept function as integral to furniture, the answer is self-evident.

Durability often is confused with quality, but in reality quality requires successful accomplishment of all design objectives . . .

Is It Comfortable?

A piece of furniture not only has to do its intended job, but it also must be comfortable and commodious. A rock will keep your backside off the ground, but a rock is neither comfortable nor convenient; a chair is both. You must be able to sleep all night in a bed, and a table must be the proper height and dimensions for its job. A coffee table's height makes it ideal for serving tea and coffee to guests, but it is uncomfortable for dining.

Will It Last?

A piece of furniture should hold up under its intended use. The life expectancies of different pieces vary and are linked to their particular functions. For example, Adirondack chairs and picnic tables that are left outdoors are not expected to last as long as a chest of drawers or a lamp stand—pieces that you hope to leave to your great-grandchildren.

Durability often is confused with quality, but in reality quality requires successful accomplishment of all design objectives, including the next one: beauty. A strong but ugly or uncomfortable chair is not good quality.

Is It Attractive?

In the days of the craft shop, appearance was the one objective that separated the journeyman from the master. By virtue of his training, the journeyman knew how to accomplish the first three objectives. He knew how to make a piece of furniture that did its job, that was comfortable to use and sturdy enough to last.

However, only the master understood form well enough to produce the masterpiece. As a furniture maker, I define a masterpiece as a decorative object that not only satisfies the first three objectives of function, comfort, and durability, but the piece also transcends time and culture.

Picture yourself entering a museum and coming upon a Ming vase. You are struck by the object and drawn to examine it. You first observe it in its entirety, standing back several paces to take in the overall statement. Next, you move closer to examine the vase in greater detail, to appreciate the finer points and to observe evidence of the craftsman's technique. The vase was made centuries before you were born and by someone living in a completely different culture. Yet it speaks to you, a viewer removed from the maker by all that time and space. It is a masterpiece.

We all want people to notice our woodworking and to appreciate the effort we invested in making it attractive. And we know intuitively that the things we make will survive us and be used by future generations. We want them to appreciate our work as well.

It is a common mistake to confuse the masterpiece with the fashionable. Both the fashionable piece and the masterpiece are appreciated in the maker's own time and culture. The appeal of the fashionable piece, however, is transitory. Trendy furniture eventually will look dated.

The masterpiece's transcendence is frequently not detectable to someone living in the period and place in which it was made. This quality emerges only as the winds of time winnow out the merely fashionable.

Look at some early issues of *Fine Woodworking*, and you'll notice the modernist furniture that was being made 27 years ago by some of the country's best known and

Function
A simple bench does nothing more than keep one's backside off the floor.

Comfort
A back and a contoured seat make the chair a more pleasant place to sit for any length of time.

Durability
Adding wedged tenons and a stretcher system will help this chair withstand many years of use and abuse.

Beauty
A masterpiece must satisfy the first three objectives while offering timeless appeal.

MASSACHUSETTS-STYLE
HIGHBOY BY RANDALL
O'DONNELL. **The appeal of this
period piece has remained
strong.**

most highly regarded woodworkers. Although the height of fashion at the time, today much of their furniture looks dated.

A Queen Anne highboy, however, is as fashionable now as it has been for a couple of centuries. Some modern furniture has generated enough universal acclaim, for enough time, to suggest similar transcendence. Sam Maloof's chairs are good candidates for masterpiece status.

Quality Furniture Meets All Objectives

The four objectives are in constant tension with each other. However, you cannot make good furniture by emphasizing one or more objectives at the expense of another.

When showing my students how to make a Windsor chair seat, I explain that the broad solid surface that supports the sitter's backside satisfies function. Also, the seat has to be nearly 2 in. thick so that it can be deeply saddled to make it comfortable and also allow deep, strong joints. However, the mass of a thick seat is in conflict with the chair's graceful lines. To resolve the conflict, the maker carves the edges and upper surface of the seat, making the slab seem thinner than it really is.

CONTEMPORARY ROCKER
BY SAM MALOOF. **This 20th-
century creation meets all
four objectives and reaches
masterpiece status.**

Another example of the tension between the four objectives is the Klismos chair, popular in the young United States and western Europe starting about 1815. The Klismos chair was developed in classical Greece and was often illustrated on Grecian urns. Although very fashionable and beautiful, the Klismos chair was not a good piece of furniture. Stretchers were not used because they did not look good when combined with graceful saber legs. However, the legs were too thin to create strong joints. The result is that few Klismos chairs lasted very long without breaking. After a decade or two of bad experience, furniture makers were forced to add stretchers to their Klismos chairs to strengthen a beautiful but weak design.

MIKE DUNBAR is a contributing editor to *Fine Woodworking* magazine.

Designing Furniture: A Survival Guide

DESIGNING A PIECE OF FURNITURE should be fun, not intimidating. Yet I know woodworkers who think nothing of building complicated jigs or mastering difficult finishes but feel lost when it comes to designing a piece of furniture truly their own.

The most important thing you can do is to train your eye. Look at furniture you like. Look in books, or go to museums, galleries, and new or antique furniture stores. Discover what appeals to you and why. In my article "Designing a Chest of Drawers" on pp. 104–108, I talk about absorbing ideas from the past and synthesizing them into your own vision. Jot down your discoveries as you make them. Measure the back of a particularly comfortable chair or the height of the seat. Keep a sketchbook of inspiring ideas; you never know how you might use some detail or rough sketch later.

Gaining confidence as a designer is more subtle than, say, learning to cut dovetails, but it's just another skill. I'll give you the loose process I follow when designing furniture and some tools and techniques that will help you along the way.

Start with What You Know

A good place to start a design is with the givens—there are always some. Say you're designing a piece with drawers. What are you going to store and how much space does it take up? This might mean measuring a stack of sweaters or sizing up particularly useful drawers you already use. If you're designing a table, consider whether it will be used next to a sofa or a bed or worked at while standing or sitting. How large does the top need to be?

Architectural Graphic Standards (John Wiley & Sons, 2000) is one place to get the starting points for a design. This book gives practical dimensions for a wide range of furniture.

BY GARRETT HACK

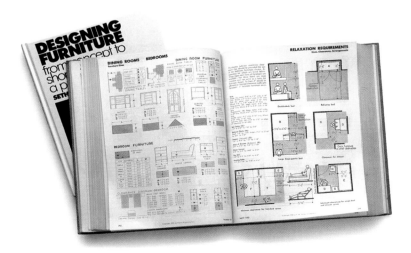

WHERE TO START. Furniture design books and architectural standard guides are good places to look for practical measurements based on average body types and ergonomic factors.

THE GOLDEN RECTANGLE

A useful proportioning rule is the golden rectangle, or golden mean, a ratio of roughly 1:1.6. It's a pleasing proportion for cabinet doors, tabletops, the front or sides of a chest of drawers, anything rectangular. You can use it to proportion the panels of a large multipaneled door, as well as the door itself. And you can stack multiple golden rectangles together—for example, a cabinet one high and two or three long.

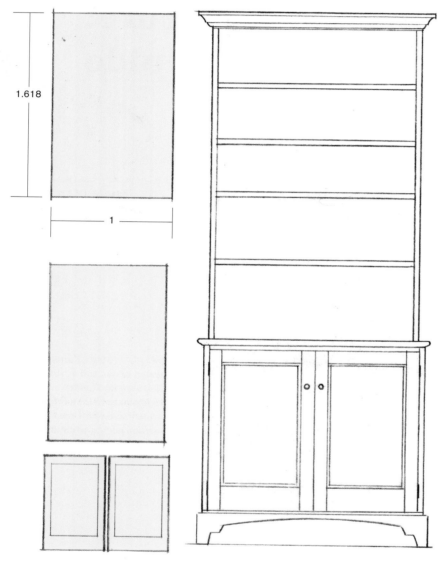

The golden rectangle was used to proportion the doors, the door panels, and the upper case of this cabinet.

Work Out the Lines and Proportions

Now, armed with (or saddled with, depending on how you look at it) the practical dimensions, work on the overall proportions and lines of the piece.

Proportion is the size relationship of the parts. It's the width of a table compared with its length or the height of each drawer face compared with the ones above and below it. But don't think only about the proportions of parts you can see; the negative spaces formed between the parts are also important. Tables and chairs create lots of negative spaces, interesting ones that can mirror and reinforce the positive, as is the case with the shapely curved back splats of 18th-century chairs.

A useful rule is the golden mean, a ratio of 1:1.618, also called the golden rectangle. It's a classical proportion for anything rectangular, such as cabinet doors, tabletops and the front or sides of a chest of drawers.

Avoid the tiresome stock lumberyard dimensions ¾ in., 1½ in., and 3½ in. in door rails and stiles, dividers between drawers, table aprons, and other highly visible parts. A variety of sizes and proportions is the most visually stimulating.

Drawings and mock-ups Typically I make lots of small sketches to get a sense of my design before making accurate full-scale drawings. Drafting full scale is always best for working out the shape of curves, details, or tricky joinery, and for recognizing potential problems before you get there. It's a useful way to see exactly what you're designing and whether the shapes and proportions are pleasing.

A full-sized drawing offers other benefits. You can transfer angles and dimensions (such as shoulder lines) directly from the drawing to the parts, making fewer errors than reading measurements off a tape. Once you get curves and contours the way you like them, you can make patterns directly from the drawing.

Drawings, however, often aren't enough to help you visualize a three-dimensional piece of furniture. At some stage a mock-up of all or part of the piece might be the best way to visualize the design. Tape together cardboard cutouts or nail together some scraps. Stand back and look at your mock-up (and drawing) from different angles. Work on something else and come back to your design with a fresh eye. Use your eyes—not your tape—to work out the dimensions of parts, such as the thickness of a tabletop, the height of the table, or the width of its apron.

Once you know what works, you can break some of the rules. Exaggerate dimensions: Design a long, narrow table or a strongly vertical chest of drawers. Instead of a progression of deepening drawers down the front of a case, add a couple of smaller ones toward the middle. Keep in mind, however, the balance of the piece. It might be solid on its feet but feel unsettling to the viewer.

Keep Construction in Mind

Aside from the practical dimensions that the design must accommodate, construction is another real-world consideration. The most ingenious design is no good if it's incredibly difficult to build. It's better (and more profitable) to build something simple that looks complicated, rather than something complicated that looks simple. So think about construction early in the design process.

Insight into how to design the joinery and build a piece often comes from experience—if you have it. If I had never made a gate-leg table, I'd look at as many examples as possible to see other makers' designs and solutions. There is no one way to build anything, but there are easier and harder ways to do it. Some ways are stronger, too.

Choose Appropriate Woods

Wood choice is both an aesthetic and technical consideration. Wood color, figure, hardness, how primary and secondary woods enhance or contrast each other, and how your wood will age are all concerns. A piece made of ash or oak, both of which have very strong grain, will be very different from the same piece made of quieter cherry or flashier bird's-eye maple. Harder woods will take fine details and hold up to wear and tear, but you may want the patina that softwoods develop with everyday use. Think through the various parts and the availability of stock wide or thick enough to make them. Of course, wood selection sometimes comes down to what you have on hand or what you can get.

Get Down to Details

While choosing woods, refining proportions, and devising construction strategies are important aspects of a design, the details are the most important—and the most elusive. These are the small touches that draw your eye and delight your senses. Some details are purely practical: a chamfer to blunt and thus protect an edge from wear. Others are purely decorative: an inlay line around a drawer. Great details can do both; for instance, beads disguise the gap

NOTHING LIKE THE REAL THING. These models of edge treatments are for the chest in the sketchbook below.

DESIGNING A BLANKET CHEST. Hack works out proportions and details in his sketchbook before moving on to full-sized drawings.

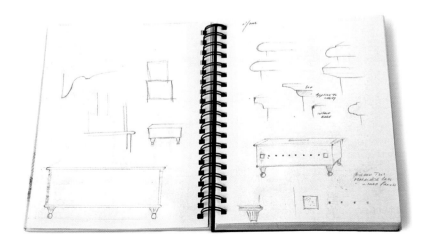

The challenge is not finding details you like—they are everywhere you look—but using them in a way that enhances rather than clutters your design.

around a door, round an edge prone to wear, and add a nicely molded outline. Some designs are rich with details. Others rely on beautiful woods and surfaces alone.

The challenge is not finding details you like—they are everywhere you look—but using them in a way that enhances rather than clutters your design. Don't give your viewers so much variety that they feel confused and overwhelmed. Treat details as variations on a theme. Use similar woods, colors, patterns, and repeating shapes and sizes to create unity in the piece. In a cherry cabinet you might use dark rosewood to pin the joints on the doors, for the knobs, and perhaps for cock beading on the drawers. A part of the crown molding could echo the bead shape.

Details are hard to see on paper but easy to mock up. Wondering about a molding shape or how big to make a chamfer? Go cut some. Test samples also give you practice making a difficult detail, can be sent to a client, and can be saved for future reference.

Part of the thrill of making something unique is leaving some things to be discovered as you build. Give yourself the flexibility to let the design evolve. Curve an edge that was to be straight, refine a leg to a more pleasing taper, deepen a rail where you can now see you need it. Even mistakes can add something to the fun; they'll force you to come up with creative solutions you just might use again.

GARRETT HACK is a professional furniture maker and contrbuting editor to *Fine Woodworking* magazine.

VARIATIONS ON A THEME.
Square pegs and rectangular wedges made of ebony work together visually in the base of a trestle table (above). A black-and-white checkered pattern is repeated in the stringing and banding on the legs of the de-milune table right, and the motif is echoed in the border of the oval inlay.

Building Without Plans

BY CRAIG VANDALL STEVENS

MOST OF US WHO WORK with wood began by making at least some things from plans. I was no exception. But working from plans can begin to feel restrictive. At some point we all wonder, "What if I designed it myself?"

Making a standing screen presents a wonderful chance to explore the design aspect of woodworking. With its straight lines and straightforward joinery, a screen presents a minimum of construction challenges, opening the way for thoughts of design. The length of the project usually can be measured in days rather than in weeks, and that can reduce the pressure of working with your own design. Still, although I've chosen to illustrate the process of design by following the development of a standing screen, the techniques I outline in this article apply not just to screens but also to any type of furniture. If you take the leap into designing your own work, I think you'll see it's a very rewarding process.

Rough Sketching Is Fine

I develop furniture ideas by sketching. I tend to make small sketches and make them quickly, especially early in the design process.

I don't want to get hung up on a lot of detail early on, when I'm trying to establish the overall form of a piece. Finding attractive proportions is one of the most challenging aspects of designing furniture, and sketching quickly enables me to explore proportions effectively. I don't think you need to be talented at drawing to design good furniture, and drawing small and quickly reduces the artistic burden.

I have a number of sketchbooks, large ones that I use in the shop and small ones that go on the road. I typically use a soft pencil, but in a pinch I'll use anything handy. I have a 9mm mechanical pencil that makes clean lines and doesn't arouse suspicion at church in my choir folder. I also have some fat drawing pencils that are great for putting the first idea for a piece down on paper. The line they leave is wide enough that I'm not tempted to draw a lot of detail, just shapes and proportions. Whatever pencil I use, I resist the temptation to erase—I just live with errant lines or work

them into the drawing. The main idea is to get some ideas down, not to make the drawing perfect. If you can't keep your fingers off the eraser, try drawing with ink.

When one of these sketches strikes an idea I like, I usually draw a number of variations of it. I'll often sketch out half a dozen or more takes on it in a sketchbook or on a large sheet of paper. Then I choose the one I like best and refine it further. I often use tracing paper to duplicate the basic shape of the piece a number of times, and then I sketch in variations on the details. Aside from saving time, tracing ensures that the part of the original drawing I like—the overall proportions, say—remains constant while I play with various details I'm less certain about.

Homemade Scale Provides Dimensions

The freehand concept drawings I've described are a great way to arrive at shapes and proportions you find pleasing. But if

THE PROPER PROPORTIONS. **Early on, while he's searching for an overall shape he likes, the author draws quickly, placing a handful of drawings on a page to make comparing them easier.**

TRACING REFINES THE SKETCH. **Once he's picked a drawing he likes, the author uses tracing paper to refine some details. Here, he traced the proportions of the frame but experimented with different ways of dividing the panels.**

How to Make a Simple Scale

An easily made paper scale enables you to assign dimensions to your drawing and make the leap from a small, freehand sketch to a full-scale mock-up.

1 The first dimension. Assign a measurement to one dimension; the author decided the screen would be 60 in. tall. Tick off the top and bottom of the piece, and the distance between them will represent 60 in.

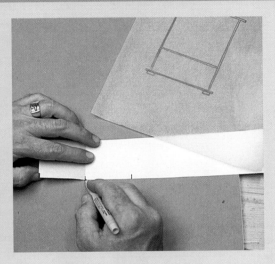

2 Fold, crease, mark. Fold the scale so that the first two tick marks meet. Then tick the crease halfway between them – it will equal 30 in.

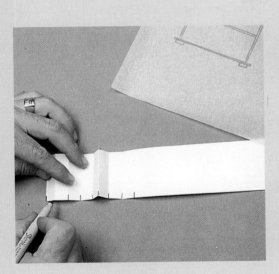

3 Keep on ticking. Continue folding the scale in half and marking the creases.

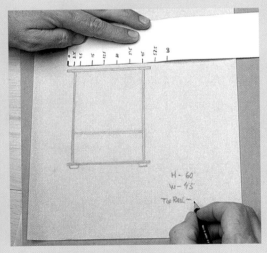

4 Rough sketch gets real dimensions. Once the scale has been marked, it can be used to measure any part of the screen.

you don't draw to scale or in accurate perspective, how do you turn a small, rough sketch into something you can build from? While a student of James Krenov's at the College of the Redwoods, I learned to use a simple homemade scale to assign dimensions to a concept sketch.

To make the scale (see the photos on p. 43), you need to assign a value to one dimension of the piece you've drawn. The measurements of all other parts will be derived from that first one. For example, in the case of my standing screen, I decided its overall height should be 60 in. On a piece of scrap paper slightly longer than my sketch of the screen, I made pencil marks that corresponded to the top and bottom of the screen. That gave me my scale: For this sketch, the distance between the two marks

would equal 60 in. I folded the paper in half with the pencil marks touching, creating a crease halfway between the marks that equaled 30 in. I made a tick mark at the crease. I folded the scale in half again and again until it was folded up like a Japanese fan. I put tick marks and the appropriate number of inches at each of the folds, and the scale was ready to use. Holding the scale horizontally across the sketch, I used it to measure the width of the screen. Such a scale can be used to determine most all the dimensions of a sketch.

Mock-ups Let You See the Piece before Building It

Once I have dimensions on my drawing, you might expect that I'd make a dimensioned shop drawing. Instead, I move at this point directly to making a mock-up of the piece. Making a mock-up is one of the most helpful steps along the path of building a piece of furniture. A full-sized mock-up allows me to see the object in three dimensions and to make informed decisions regarding proportions and size. A full-sized drawing of a piece doesn't give me anything like the impact of a mock-up. It also locks me into decisions on detailing before I'm ready. I generally don't make a scale model, either, because it doesn't provide the sense of physical presence that a mock-up does.

My mock-ups aren't built to last. I use common materials (for the screen I used 2x stock for the frame and kraft paper for the panels) and the quickest possible joinery (drywall screws, brads). I want a mock-up to be as simple as possible to make and easily modified again and again until I'm comfortable with the design. I probably spent about an hour and a half building the screen mock-up. The less time it takes to build one, the more inclined I'll be to alter something I don't like. And that's the whole point of a mock-up.

I use my first mock-up, like my first sketches, to determine the overall shape and proportions of a piece. When I had the first

SIZING UP THE FRAME. Before determining any of the details, the author considers the overall proportions of the screen and the placement of the crossbar.

mock-up of the screen in front of me, I saw that it was far wider than it appeared in the sketch. What had looked nicely balanced on paper was somewhat clumsy in three dimensions and full size. I made decisions regarding the overall width of the screen (I decided it needed narrowing), the thickness of the lower rail (it needed thinning), and the way the feet relate to the rest of the screen (they needed to be less clunky).

Implementing such changes is easy. I don't need a second mock-up; I simply unscrew the first one (or unclamp it if I haven't yet driven the screws) and use the chopsaw to shorten some members and the bandsaw to shave a bit off the elements that look too heavy. With the bandsaw, I'm not measuring and taking off specific amounts, just taking off enough to make a difference visually. I generally start with all of the parts a little oversized and work down from there. I had roughed out a few extra blanks for feet, and I quickly cut out a couple of new possibilities on the bandsaw. I put two different feet on the mock-up to compare likely candidates.

When I finish a mock-up, I take it into the house and live with it a while. I place it so it's the first thing I see when I walk into the room. Over the next few days, I try to let it surprise me when I enter the room. The first impression I have of the proportions is telling. It's not a life-changing moment of clarity. It's usually just a quick thought like, "It's too tall," or "The feet are too fat." I pay attention to these impressions, because they are uncluttered by logic, analysis, formulas, and so on. Everyone has such responses, but it may take some coaxing to get yourself to trust them.

With this new input, I take apart the mock-up, make the changes, reassemble it and take another look. At this stage, I might also add some fine detailing to the mock-up. (Before this, I have avoided including details such as subtle textures and reveals because I find them distracting early on.)

GET ME OUT OF THE SHOP.
Placing a mock-up in a room for a few days can help clarify the design's strengths and weaknesses.

The new proportions may result in the need to fiddle with the dimensions of other parts, but the mock-up is definitely making headway. Overall, I find that a mock-up provides an enjoyable and reassuring way to develop and refine a design.

How I Design a Carving

The screen's panels provide a wonderful canvas for the free-flowing type of carving I do. To design a carving, I use sketching techniques very similar to those used to design the screen itself. I start small, drawing on the panels of my thumbnail sketch of the screen. Working small helps me see the carving design as a whole and keeps me from getting bogged down in details.

Once I have an idea that works well with the screen design, I begin sketching full scale. I use kraft or butcher's paper from a wide roll to make the drawing. I'll prop up a piece of plywood and tape the paper to it so that I can draw while standing. I keep the small sketch nearby for reference as I work full size.

I use a soft pencil, and often instead of holding it the way I would to write, I hold it almost flat under my palm. This produces a wider, bolder line and permits my arm and hand to move in comfortable arcs, creating graceful lines more easily.

I pin the finished sketch to the mock-up so I can stand back and see it framed in the screen. Sometimes after seeing it in place, I make changes to the drawing to create a better sense of balance with the screen.

Once I'm satisfied with the sketch, I'll lay out the real panels in the order they'll take in the screen and transfer the design to the panels with carbon paper. Then the carving can begin.

One important general tip on carving design: Resist the urge to fill the whole space. Leaving some space uncarved can significantly increase the impact of the carving. Particularly when you are working a large surface in this style of chip carving, the old maxim applies: Less really is more.

CRAIG VANDALL STEVENS lives and works wood in Sunbury, Ohio.

TO THE BIG BOARD. A piece of plywood propped on a chair (another old mock-up) serves as an easel for sketching the carving design. The author uses a fat pencil to produce a flowing line.

THE FINISHED PIECE. The author developed the screen's pleasing proportions, careful detailing, and calm presence without benefit of elaborate shop drawings.

Creating Working Drawings

FOR MUCH OF MY WOODWORKING career, I dreaded the drawing stage of a project. It was always a daunting, tedious process that only put off the true fun—shaping real wood into real objects. After erasing a misplaced or poorly drawn line for the umpteenth time, I'd often think that I could have built the darn thing in the time it took to do the drawings. Considering the way I was producing drawings, I was probably right.

Today, however, I thoroughly enjoy the drawing process, and I relish seeing my ideas first come to life on paper. I've learned to appreciate the unlimited design freedom afforded by freehand concept sketching, as well as the ability to express my ideas clearly and precisely with more refined drawing techniques. The difference in my attitude came from learning to use the right tools and techniques. In this article, I'll share what I've learned about materials

BY JIM TOLPIN

LOOSE CONCEPT SKETCHING FOSTERS creativity and allows you to refine your rough idea to the point where you're ready to create a three-view drawing and then an isometric projection. From there it's not all that far to full-scale drawings and to creating something with wood. The time spent getting a drawing right will pay for itself many times over.

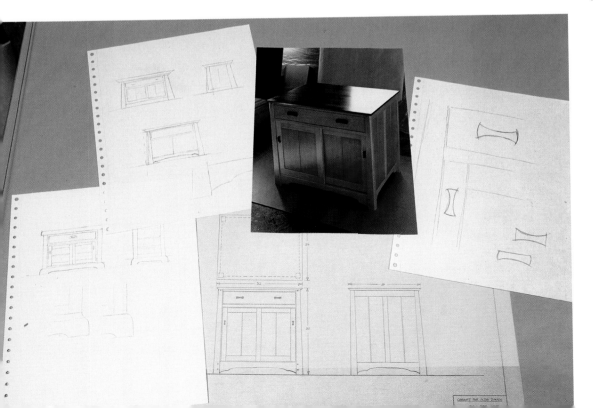

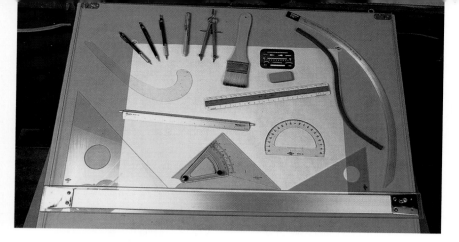

DRAWING SUPPLIES USED BY the author include, clockwise from lower left, a 45° to 45° angle template, a metal architect's rule, a ship's curve (a large version of a French curve), mechanical pencils in three sizes (3mm, 5mm, and 7mm), a pencil-style eraser, a compass, a dust brush, an eraser shield, a pink eraser, a flat architect's rule, a lead flexible curve, a plastic adjustable curve, an orange 30° to 60° angle template, a protractor, and an adjustable angle template.

and techniques and explain how you can take your design ideas from rough, raw images to refined, scale working drawings. Here's an overview.

From Concept Sketch to Orthographic Drawing

I begin the drawing process by first creating a series of concept sketches that show the object in a roughly accurate perspective view—in other words, the way the object would appear to your eyes. Choosing the sketch that comes closest to my design goal, I commit its dimensions to a scaled-down, three-view drawing—an orthographic projection. This gives me a way to see the parts of the piece in their true proportion to one another. But because this type of drawing limits me to viewing each face independ-

ently from the others, I will often go on to draw an assembled view of the drawing—an isometric projection. This drawing shows me how all the parts relate to one another, and it gives me an accurate feel for how a piece will look when it's built.

Concept Sketching

This is where the fun begins. You get your first look at the project-to-be, and you can work out the bugs in the overall look of the piece without laboring over the details. Approach concept sketching by giving your hand free rein to draw and redraw any inspiration that comes to mind. This is not the time to worry about crisp lines, perfect symmetry, properly scaled proportions, or fair curves. You can take care of all that later when you produce the mechanical drawings. Do not, however, go on from sketching to drafting until you have something you really like. It's too time-consuming to make major design changes at the drafting stage.

A ring-bound artist's sketchbook is the best place to do your concept sketching. Choose a soft (#2 or #2½) lead pencil with a pink-tipped eraser. Avoid using harder pencils because their lines are difficult to erase from typical sketchbook paper. Keep a

Fig. 1: Lines Used in Working Drawings

Lines of different thickness help to distinguish different meanings in working drawings. Here are some of the most common line types.

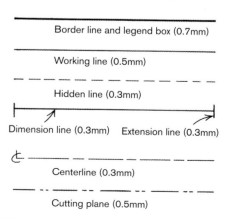

Border line and legend box (0.7mm)

Working line (0.5mm)

Hidden line (0.3mm)

Dimension line (0.3mm)   Extension line (0.3mm)

Centerline (0.3mm)

Cutting plane (0.5mm)

Fig. 2: Setting Out a Three-View Orthographic Drawing

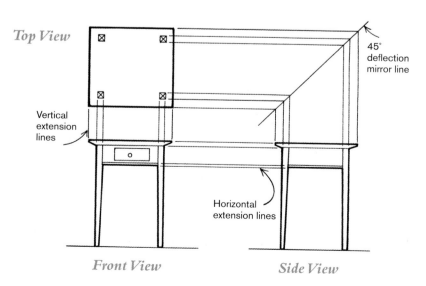

Top View

45° deflection mirror line

Vertical extension lines

Horizontal extension lines

Front View

Side View

half-dozen or so well-sharpened pencils handy as you sketch. You don't want a dull pencil to interrupt the flow of your creative juices. Hold the pencil lightly, keeping your wrist loose and flexible. When sketching out a long line, allow your arm to move with your hand. And finally, get in the habit of turning the sketchbook to accommodate the natural sweep of your wrist when drawing angled lines.

One of the benefits of doing freehand concept sketches is that you can easily create a series of "what-if" views. Instead of redrawing the form over and over again, simply trace it onto a piece of translucent paper, leaving out the areas that will be changed in the what-if views. Or you can photocopy as many basic outlines as you'd like, and then flesh them out with your new design ideas.

Once you have settled on a concept sketch that comes closest to representing your idea, it's time to assign some dimensions to the project. By setting out the design to scale in a mechanical drawing, you can see clearly how the size and shape of components relate to one another. Methods and sequences of joinery also become more obvious. These working drawings are a bridge between your freehand concept sketches and a master cut list.

Equipment— Buying the Right Stuff

Luckily, the type of equipment a woodworker needs to produce adequate working drawings is relatively simple and inexpensive. Unless you do a lot of room-sized architectural millwork, a 2-ft. by 3-ft. board will provide plenty of space for rendering projects in a suitable scale. This board can be nothing more than a flat piece of plywood set on a desktop, but to make it more comfortable to work at, tilt up the back of the board 3 in. to 4 in. Adding a piece of drafting-board vinyl (available through most office-supply stores) smooths the drawing

Fig. 3: Producing a Side View of an Angled Side

Problem: You cannot use a mirror line to project side of top view to baseline because distance B is foreshortened to look as though it's less than distance A.

Solution: Use an architect's rule or a compass to measure distance A and transfer distance directly to horizontal line extended over from front view. Drop lines to baseline from distance marks.

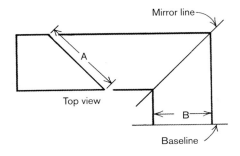
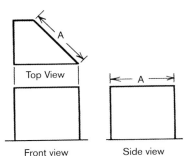

surface and will allow holes left behind by compass points to self-heal. To pinch pennies, you can cover the board with a ⅛-in. sheet of corrugated cardboard, but pin holes and pencil grooves will soon telegraph through to the drawings.

You can draw consistently parallel lines and angles with templates and a simple T-square, but I highly recommend spending a bit more money and setting yourself up with a sliding parallel rule fixed to a cable run along either side of the board.

You can further reduce drawing-board madness by using only high-grade (16 to 20 lb.), fine-grained vellum paper for mechanical drawings. Unlike sketch paper, vellum erases easily with a standard pink gum eraser, leaving behind a smooth, smudge-free surface. The vellum is also translucent, letting you trace over prototype sketches, speeding the drawing of repetitive elements.

Other pieces of equipment you'll need for mechanical drawing include the following:

Pencils Forget wood pencils. They're time-consuming, messy to sharpen, and because their width changes as they dull, they make lines of uneven thickness. Instead, get a set of three mechanical pencils (3mm, 5mm, and 7mm) and use an HB grade lead. It will dull quickly, but it will produce a dark line

Fig. 4: Setting in Dimension Lines

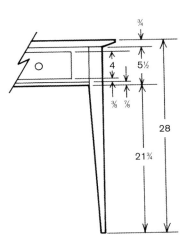

Note: The overall dimension—the height in this case—is drawn to the outside of all other dimensions. In general, the smallest dimensions are kept closest to the object.

that reproduces well in a copy machine, eliminating the need to ink the drawing.

Erasers On vellum paper, the classic pink gum eraser works as well as any. To make fine corrections, use pencil-type erasers in conjunction with eraser shields.

Ruler I use an architect's scale rule for laying out dimensioned lines. I prefer a flat ruler with eight scales rather than the twelve-scale triangular rulers, which I find more difficult to mark dimensions from. To keep the edges of a rule smooth and clean, use it only to mark dimensions, never as a straightedge for drawing lines—that's what a parallel rule and angle templates are for.

Angle templates To start out, get an 8-in. 45° to 45°, an 8-in. 30° to 60° and an adjustable-angle template. Later, you'll want to add a 4-in. version of this set for drawing small details. I like my templates in green or orange, so I can readily find them amid the papers strewn about the drawing board.

Shape templates Circles, ellipses, squares, and rectangles, as well as a variety of other shapes, are available on templates. I also use French-curve templates and their larger cousins, ship's curves, to draw in curves of progressively changing radii.

Adjustable curves To draw curves between fixed points, I use either a flexible lead bar or a plastic slip curve. If the curve is very large, I'll bend a ³⁄₁₆-in.-sq. length of straight-grained wood to the marks while I trace a line against its edge.

Protractor I use a 4-in.-radius protractor to draw angles from a baseline.

Compass A pencil compass is useful for drawing circles.

Drafting Basics

Unless you move on from woodworking to designing and building space shuttles, you won't need to learn more than the most basic drafting skills and conventions to produce quick, accurate and easy-to-read working drawings. The skills are mostly common sense: Make sure your board is free of lead and eraser debris before taping paper to it. Align the bottom of the paper to the parallel rule, and then secure it to the board with a small piece of tape in each corner. Keep a scrap piece of paper between your hand and the drawing to avoid smudging your work. And never wipe away eraser debris with your hand—always use a brush.

Once you establish a baseline, draw any degree angle to it using either angle templates or a protractor and straightedge. Begin the angled line precisely on a dimension mark by first holding the pencil to the mark and then sliding the template or straightedge to it. If you reverse this process, parallax can play tricks on your eyes, causing you to misjudge the placement of the pencil. Draw out a waver-free line by tilting the pencil slightly into the

Fig. 5: Creating an Isometric Projection

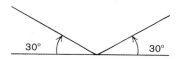

Step 1: Create two angled baselines, each at 30° to your original horizontal baseline.

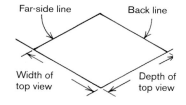

Step 2: Draw in the "footprint" of the top view along the angled baselines. Extend the view back into the isometric projection by drawing the back and the far-side lines. Keep these lines parallel to the angled baselines.

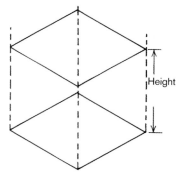

Step 3: Establish the actual top view by extending vertical lines up from the corners of the footprint. Measure up along the line to the overall height of the front view. Draw in the outline of the top view parallel to the angled baselines.

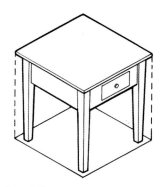

Step 4: Now simply draw in the piece of furniture using the dimension from your orthographic drawing.

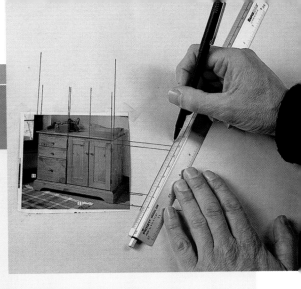

Developing a Three-View Drawing from a Photograph

It's possible to develop scaled views of a piece of furniture from nothing more than a photograph. It helps, of course, if you know the overall dimensions of the piece, but some detective work—such as scaling dimensions from familiar objects in the photo—can often provide enough clues. The picture should be as free from distortion as possible (no wide-angle shots) and should offer a three-quarter view, which lets you see the front, side, and top of the piece.

To determine the dimensions of doors, drawers, and other elements of the piece, affix the photo to the center of a piece of vellum paper with double-faced tape. Use a straightedge to extend lines out from the overall width and height of the piece. Then lay an architect's rule between the two lines that represent the overall dimension of the piece (see the photo at right). Usually, you'll have to angle the rule to get the scaled dimension to fall between the lines. Use whatever scale allows you to correlate the overall dimensions of the piece to a reasonable, divisible section of the rule.

Draw this angled reference line, and then extend over the outlines of the internal elements. To find their dimensions, simply consult the same scale on the rule. Repeat this procedure to find the dimension of elements within the other planes of the photograph. Once you've established all the dimensions for all elements of the piece, use this information to create a three-view drawing of the piece from which you can create a cut list.

corner formed between the edge of the template and the paper.

A mechanical drawing is nothing more than a happy meeting of lines that indicate the outlines of an object and where measurements are being made to. Unless these lines vary in some way, however, the drawing can be difficult to read. Figure 1 on p. 48 shows how lines with different meanings are conventionally rendered in mechanical drawings. Note that dimensions are not given a unit symbol. This would only crowd the drawing. Instead, a note in the legend box tells you what units are represented by the dimension numbers.

A Three-View Drawing

The first type of working drawing I produce from a concept sketch (or from dimensions taken from a photo or some other source) is a three-view (orthographic) projection. I tape a copy of my final concept sketch (or a combination of sketches) to the top of my drafting board and then attach a piece of vellum to the board. I draw a thick (.7mm) borderline around the perimeter and a legend box in the lower right-hand corner. Within this box, I record my name and a copyright symbol (©), followed by the date and the name of the client, if any. If the piece has a name, or if it is a reproduction, I will title it accordingly. Finally, I indicate the scale and units of measurement used in the drawing.

Unless the project is very large, such as a floor-to-ceiling entertainment center, I use ¼ in. to represent 1 in. This reduction allows me to fit the front, side and top views onto one sheet without creating a cluttered drawing that's difficult to read. I use two scales on my architect's rule to lay out the dimensions: the ¼ scale and the 3 scale. Although the ¼ scale is useful for representing full-inch increments, its divisions are in twelfths (because this scale is designed primarily to equate ¼ in. to 1 ft.), which is not a convenient scale for fractions of an inch. For fractions, I use the 3 scale, where a ¼-in. segment is broken down into eight divisions, each representing ⅛ in.

After drawing a horizontal baseline about 2 in. up from the lower border of the paper, I lay out the rough positions of the three views with a light pencil line. As a right-hander, I find it more comfortable to draw from left to right, so I place the front view in the lower left-hand corner of the drawing, the top view above and the side view to the right (see Figure 2 on p. 48).

I do the front view first, constantly referring to the concept sketch (or to dimension notes) as I draw in the outline of the form with light lines. I generally trust my eye to judge whether proportions are correct. When I'm satisfied with this light pencil rendering, I darken in the outline with 0.5mm working lines.

I draw the top view next, extending lines up vertically from the front view to define the widths. Next I create the side view. Only one is necessary unless the piece is asymmetrical. With the front and top views already completed, the dimensions of the side view are already established in the drawing. To draw this view, I need only extend over the outlines of the other two views until they intersect over the baseline to the right of the front view. As you can see in Figure 3 on p. 49, I reflect the top view's extension lines down to the baseline with a 45° mirror line.

A note of caution: reflecting extension lines from a top view across a mirror line works only if the side of an object is perpendicular to its front. At any other angle, reflected lines create a foreshortened view. Although this is technically correct in a true orthographic projection, it makes more sense to draw the angled side so that the length of its side remains true to scale. Skip the top view reflection and scale the depth

dimensions directly from the architect's rule or with a compass (see Figure 3).

I finish the three-view drawing by penciling in all my dimensions, working my way out from the smallest elements of the components, to the components themselves, to the overall size of the structure (see Figure 4 on p. 49). Then I draw in the fine details shown in my concept sketches: curved or molded corners or edges, knobs, pulls, and the like. I rarely bother with cross sections or detail blowups in my three-view drawings. Instead, I wait to do these on a full-scale rendering. If I need this kind of information, I want it actual size, so I can transfer the information directly onto a story pole, or measuring stick. I do label all the parts on the three-view drawing, so I can refer to them in the bill of materials and cut lists.

From Three-View Drawing to Isometric Projection

The advantage of an isometric projection is that it shows you how the various faces of an object will relate to one another. And because an isometric doesn't diminish or foreshorten dimensions as does a vanishing-point perspective drawing, all the views of this working drawing remain true to scale, making it simple to draw and easy to take off scaled dimensions (see Figure 5 on p. 50).

Once I've created the isometric cube that establishes the perimeter of the piece of furniture I'm drawing, I fill in the three views by transferring scaled measurements from the three-view drawing, being careful to orient the lines parallel to the 30° baselines. You may find it helpful to place isometric grid paper under the vellum as an aid to sketching in some details. When you're finished filling in the details of the piece, erase the extension lines used to raise the structure, and you're done.

JIM TOLPIN is a writer and woodworker in Port Townsend, Wash.

Drafting Basics

BY PHILIP C. LOWE

MANY FOLKS CONSIDER time spent at the drawing table to be time taken away from woodworking. They think that unless they're cutting wood, no progress is being made. Actually both time and material are being saved, not to mention a lot of head-scratching.

The first of any piece of furniture is always the most labor-intensive. To be successful, both design and construction must be ironed out beforehand, so I do a full-size drawing for every new piece I build. By laying out a design at full scale, you get a better sense of its proportions and size. Also, patterns and templates for curved parts can be made directly from an accurate drawing, which means you don't have to redraw parts that were sketched out at a smaller scale.

The full-size drawing typically includes three views and a few other important details and sections. The number of views and sections needed is determined by the complexity of the design.

The Basic Tools for Drawing

My drawing table is a 4-ft. by 8-ft. angled surface covered with a vinyl mat and equipped with a cable-controlled parallel rule. But all you need to make accurate drawings is a large, smooth surface (like Baltic birch plywood or medium-density fiberboard) with two parallel edges to run a T-square against. Add a ruler, a set of triangles, a white plastic eraser, an erasing shield, and a dusting brush, and you're off.

For best results, I recommend hard pencil lead and special drafting paper. I use a mechanical pencil and drafting vellum called Charprint 916H, which I purchase in 42-in.-wide rolls.

The two tools used most often in drafting are designed to do the two most funda-

Everything You Need in a Single Drawing

A full-size drawing helped Lowe determine critical design and construction aspects for this side table. Before putting tool to wood, he worked out the curves of the rails, the taper of the legs, the overhang of the top, the joinery, and a precise cut list.

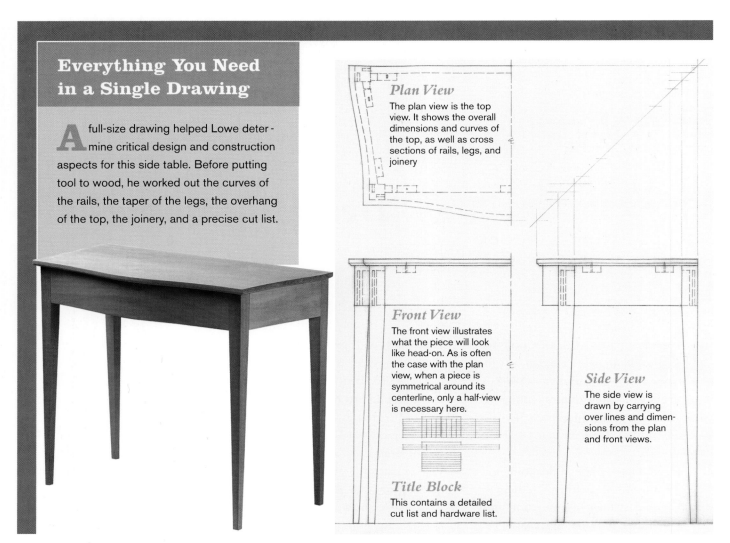

Plan View
The plan view is the top view. It shows the overall dimensions and curves of the top, as well as cross sections of rails, legs, and joinery

Front View
The front view illustrates what the piece will look like head-on. As is often the case with the plan view, when a piece is symmetrical around its centerline, only a half-view is necessary here.

Side View
The side view is drawn by carrying over lines and dimensions from the plan and front views.

Title Block
This contains a detailed cut list and hardware list.

A Glossary of Lines

Illustrators and draftspeople use a variety of line styles in drawings to make them easier to understand.

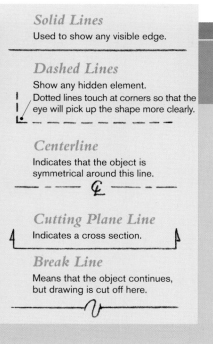

Solid Lines
Used to show any visible edge.

Dashed Lines
Show any hidden element. Dotted lines touch at corners so that the eye will pick up the shape more clearly.

Centerline
Indicates that the object is symmetrical around this line.

Cutting Plane Line
Indicates a cross section.

Break Line
Means that the object continues, but drawing is cut off here.

mental operations. The first tool, the T-square or parallel rule, is used to draw horizontal lines. Second is the triangle: Either the 30-60-90 or the 45-45-90 is used for drawing vertical lines perpendicular to the horizontals. These triangles also are used to draw common angles measuring 30°, 45°, and 60°. A straightedge is important because it can be used to draw a straight line at any angle, such as the tapers on legs. A T-square flipped onto its back (so it will lie flat) makes a workable straightedge.

The compass is the tool of choice for regular curves. I draw irregular curves freehand, which can be more pleasing to the eye than a curve made using a compass or French curve. I smooth out these freehand lines with a tool called an adjustable ship curve.

When drawing freehand curves, the lines tend to be a bit heavy. I clean them up using an erasing shield, a thin sheet of metal with various shapes cut into it. By covering the portion of the line that you want to save with the erasing shield, you can erase the exposed part and clean up unsightly stray lines with a white plastic eraser.

Then there is the pencil lead that you use. My choice is No. 4 hard lead, which is not likely to smear but still makes a clear line. If you use a pencil like this, you will need a lead pointer, which is a fancy term for a special sharpener.

If you happen to remove the drawing from the board and discover that you need to add something, you can place the paper back on the board, match any horizontal line with the T-square edge and tape the drawing back in place.

Designing a Side Table in Three Views

To help you understand the drawing process and its advantages, I'll draw (and design) a basic side table with a curved front and sides. There are many design and construction decisions to make on a table like this—overall proportions, curves, tapers, joinery—and all of these details can be drawn on paper before making the first cut in valuable stock.

Once I have the paper taped to the board, the best place to start is the floor. A simple horizontal line, a couple of inches up from the bottom of the paper, does the trick. From here, I think about the overall dimensions of the table: height, width, and depth. The height is based on the type of table it is. I draw a light, horizontal line at 29 in. to 30 in., the standard height for a side table, which most likely will have a vase or lamp on it. These two lines are the beginning of the front and side views.

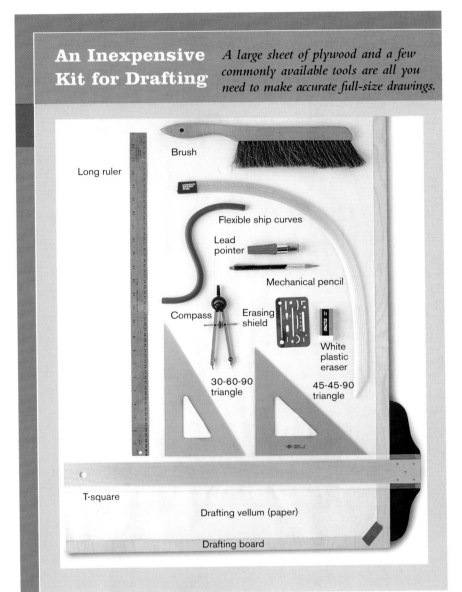

An Inexpensive Kit for Drafting
A large sheet of plywood and a few commonly available tools are all you need to make accurate full-size drawings.

Long ruler

Brush

Flexible ship curves

Lead pointer

Mechanical pencil

Compass

Erasing shield

White plastic eraser

30-60-90 triangle

45-45-90 triangle

T-square

Drafting vellum (paper)

Drafting board

Next, in the space above the front view, I draw a light rectangle that represents the size of the tabletop. This is the top, or plan, view. These few lines establish the overall size.

Half views are enough
Once I am happy with the proportions, I pencil in the centerline on the plan view and carry it down to the front view. On most pieces of furniture, including this one, only a half view is necessary for the front and plan views. I draw everything to the left of the centerline. The side view will show the entire piece.

Step 1
Draw Overall Dimensions and Curves

Determine the height of the tabletop and get an idea of its overall size. Then draw the actual curved edges on the left of the centerline. Only half of the table needs to be drawn in the front and plan views.

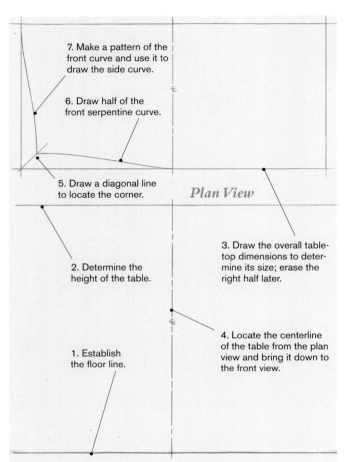

7. Make a pattern of the front curve and use it to draw the side curve.

6. Draw half of the front serpentine curve.

5. Draw a diagonal line to locate the corner.

Plan View

3. Draw the overall table-top dimensions to determine its size; erase the right half later.

2. Determine the height of the table.

4. Locate the centerline of the table from the plan view and bring it down to the front view.

1. Establish the floor line.

Front View

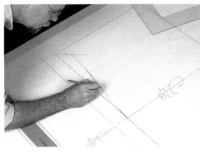

DRAW HALF OF THE FRONT CURVE. Sketch it out freehand, trusting your eye.

SMOOTH THE CURVE. Use a flexible ship curve to create a fair, even profile.

MAKE A PLYWOOD PATTERN. Poke a series of holes through the paper to transfer the pattern to thin plywood.

DRAW SYMMETRICAL CURVES. Use the pattern to draw a matching serpentine curve on the side rail and to lay out the actual workpieces.

These half views have a few important advantages. They not only mean a smaller drawing and less work, but they also guarantee symmetry. I make a half template for the serpentine curve across the front, and simply flip it to lay out the other side. This is much easier than trying to draw the entire curve and match both sides. Also, the same curve is used on the sides.

I draw half of the serpentine curve across the front in the plan view. I draw this line freehand, working to get a curve that is pleasing to my eye.

I made this tabletop twice as wide as it is deep, allowing two important things to happen. One, the same half-serpentine

curve pattern for the front can be used for the side. Two, the entire table can be doubled, turning it into a card table with an identical serpentine rail on all four sides.

After drawing the curve for the front, I use a piece of ⅛-in.-thick plywood to make a pattern of the curve by laying the plywood underneath the drawing and pricking holes along the line, through the paper and into the plywood. I saw out the pattern and smooth it with a spokeshave and sandpaper. I can use it as a template for doing the rest of the drawing, and when building the table in the shop.

Step 2 Size the Legs and Rails

After choosing the overhang of the tabletop, draw the legs in the plan view, transfer the leg and tabletop edges to the front view, and add the tabletop chamfer and hidden lines for the rails.

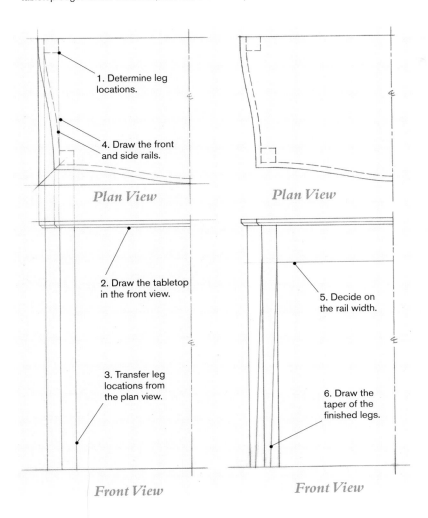

1. Determine leg locations.

4. Draw the front and side rails.

Plan View

Plan View

2. Draw the tabletop in the front view.

5. Decide on the rail width.

3. Transfer leg locations from the plan view.

6. Draw the taper of the finished legs.

Front View

Front View

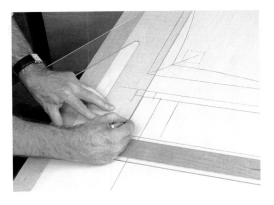

TRANSFER LINES FROM THE PLAN view to the front view. Use a long triangle to carry down the table-top and leg edges.

DRAW THE RAILS IN THE TOP VIEW. Use the overhang dimension to offset the curved rail evenly from the curved tabletop. Lowe is using a triangular scale, but any ruler will do.

The overhang determines the table base Looking at the front and plan views, I decide the overhang of the tabletop. For this table, a slight overhang will keep the tabletop from hiding the rail and will accentuate the matching curves in both. At this point, I also determine the thickness of the tabletop and draw it into the front and plan views. A heavy chamfer under the edge lightens the look.

The overhang dimension is used to position the legs and rails in the plan view. At this point, I consider the width and thickness of the legs and draw them. Now, using a triangle, I project the dimensions of the

legs down into the front view. I also continue these light lines to the floor, which end up forming the rectangles of stock from which the legs will be sawn.

On this traditional table, I keep the rails flush with the legs. It's easier to build an inset rail, but a flush rail creates a smooth flow around the corner for a more high-style look. To draw the curved rails in the plan view, you need a hidden line that is offset evenly from the curve of the top. The overhang of the tabletop is ⅜ in. I mark this offset from the tabletop edge in a dozen or so places and then use a ship curve to draw a

Step 3 Draw the Side View

All of the information necessary to complete the side view is incorporated in the plan and front views.

NOW FILL IN THE SIDE VIEW. Carry over horizontal lines from the front view and transfer the other dimensions from the plan view using a 45° line or simply by measuring.

To transfer dimensions from the plan view to the side view, draw a line at a 45° angle and project lines across and then down.

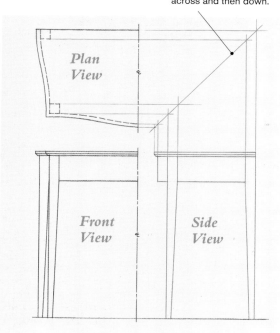

Plan View

Front View

Side View

Step 4 Add Joinery and Title Block

Design the joinery in the plan view, find the rail thicknesses, fill in the front and side views and add the title block.

FIGURE OUT THE SIDE RAIL'S THICKNESS. Start with a construction line to determine the outside edge of the rail stock, then offset a parallel line from that to find the inside edge of the rail.

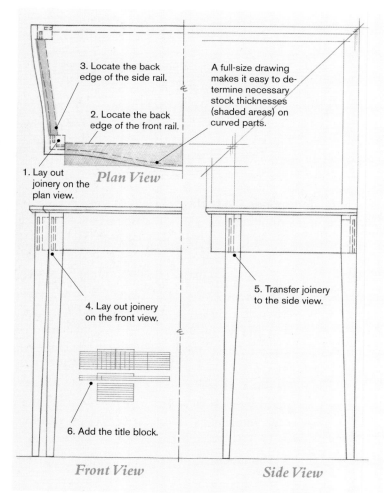

3. Locate the back edge of the side rail.

2. Locate the back edge of the front rail.

A full-size drawing makes it easy to determine necessary stock thicknesses (shaded areas) on curved parts.

1. Lay out joinery on the plan view.

Plan View

5. Transfer joinery to the side view.

4. Lay out joinery on the front view.

6. Add the title block.

Front View

Side View

smooth curve for the rail. Next, I pick a pleasing width for the front rail.

Jumping back to the legs, I consider how they should be tapered—on two sides or four? Having decided that a two-sided taper looks best on this table, I lay out the amount of taper at the floor line and locate one end of a long straightedge on the drawing at that point. The other end goes on a point about ⅛ in. below the rail, where I generally start my tapers.

Develop the side view So far, I only have worked on the front and plan views. To create a side view, I project lines from the front view and take the horizontal dimensions from the plan view. Until now, only the external lines of the table have been addressed, so if any of the proportions need to be changed, this is the time to do it. The white eraser will make clean work of it. Once I'm satisfied, it's time to fill in the joinery.

Joinery determines the thickness of the rails First, in the plan view, I fill in the locations of the mortises and tenons. Then I can draw the back edge of the rail, determining its overall thickness.

On smaller tables like this, I keep the front cheeks of the tenons ¼ in. back from the outside of the leg and use a ¼-in.-thick tenon. These locations allow long mortises to fit inside the leg without touching one another and weakening the leg.

The first step on the plan view is to draw the back rail ¾ in. thick with the standard ¼-in.-thick tenon. Then, after drawing the joinery on the front rail in the plan view, I can draw the horizontal line indicating the back of that piece, and a clear view of the stock develops. I can determine easily that it must be 2⅜ in. thick to contain the curve.

The side rails can be taken from a thinner piece of stock by drawing a construction line from the outside edge of the curve to the rail's front shoulder, and then drawing a line parallel to that one to indicate the overall thickness of the part.

Project joinery to the front and side views
Now carry the tenon thicknesses and lengths down to the front view and in turn to the side view. One last decision that needs to be made regarding the tenons is their width and the size of any top or bottom shoulders to make the table resist racking. I think giving the tenons a ¼-in. shoulder at the top and no shoulder at the bottom is enough. It is easier to align the bottom edge of the rails to each other without a shoulder to deal with, making it easier to apply any banding that might run around the bottom edge of the rails and across the legs.

If there is no shoulder at the top, an open mortise is created and the strength of the leg is compromised. It wouldn't stand up to an accidental kick or a whack from a wayward vacuum cleaner.

The last element that I place on the drawing is the title block, which contains both a cut list and a hardware list. I refer to the drawing many times during construction, keeping myself organized and avoiding costly errors.

PHILIP C. LOWE runs a woodworking school and makes period furniture at his shop in Beverly, Mass.

What Information Goes into a Title Block?

The title block is an important last step. It contains rough and finished stock dimensions, listing wood species, and comments for each part, as well as a hardware list, the date, and the maker's name and address.

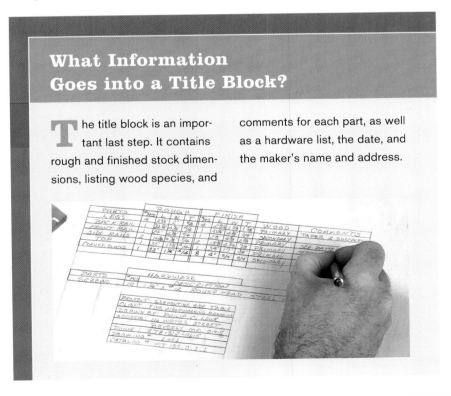

Models Help Projects Succeed

BY JAN ZAITLIN

BIG OR SMALL, MODELS help refine design. The author uses three kinds of models to help her visualize furniture projects before they are built. Full-size mock-ups can be assembled quickly with cardboard and straight pins, as she does here.

I'M A BIG FAN OF MAKING MODELS and mock-ups before I move on to a finished piece of furniture. Whether the prototypes are cardboard or foam, full size or one-eighth scale, they help solve a long list of furnituremaking problems. Models are good for demonstrating knockdown features and can help me decide what construction techniques to use. Clients love models because visualizing the real thing from drawings can be difficult; models can show clients how finished pieces will look in their intended room settings. Even if I'm building a project for myself, a quick model can prevent disappointments later.

I use several types of models, and the applications and the materials for each vary. I have three favorites: the quick, full-scale mock-up, what I call the scale appearance model, and the full-size detail mock-up like the one in the photo below.

A Quick, Full-Scale Mock-Up

A mock-up is a quick, inexpensive, full-scale, approximation of the completed piece. The purpose is to catch any obvious mistakes in proportion. I usually build one right after I have my design concept drawn, dimensioned, and approved. The mock-up shouldn't take more than an hour to construct and should be taken to the site. There, I can tell if the finished piece will be the right size for the intended space, if it blocks too much light or if its position or dimensions will cause some other unexpected problem, such as limiting the swing of a door. If the project is a dining table, I can place chairs around the mock-up to see if it makes the room seem too crowded, allows room for serving platters, and seats the required number of people comfortably.

I use inexpensive materials that can be worked quickly. Mock-ups need not be pretty. For most projects, I use corrugated

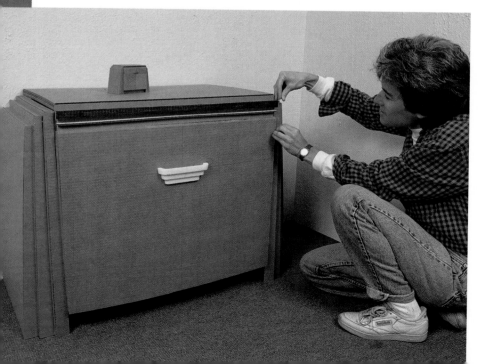

cardboard, which can be used for curved as well as angular projects because I can bend it with the "grain." And I can draw on it with a pencil or marker to suggest details.

Sometimes the appropriate mock-up material is foam board, polystyrene foam sandwiched between smooth paper. Foam board looks cleaner than cardboard, and it doesn't have the strong grain that corrugated cardboard has. It is available at art and architectural supply stores and comes in a range of thicknesses (⅛ in., ³⁄₁₆ in., ½ in.) and in sheet sizes up to 4 ft. by 8 ft.

Both foam board and cardboard are easily cut with a utility knife. I use a cordless hot-melt glue gun for quick assembly. On those occasions where hot-melt glue is not appropriate (it can be messy and thick), I have used a quick-drying white glue called Elmer's® Tacky Glue. I also use a variety of tapes including repositionable tape, which is good for changing things around. Check the adhesives section in art or graphic supply stores.

A handy fastener for butt joining is an ordinary straight pin, the kind used by tailors to hold fabric together. These are available at fabric stores and often at grocery and drug stores. Straight pins are great for making a knockdown mock-up (see the photo on the facing page).

For more sculptural applications, such as a chair or lamp base, or wherever it is important to show mass, I use rigid blue foam (extruded polystyrene). It is used in construction as insulation and comes in 2-ft. by 8-ft. sheets, 1 in. and 2 in. thick. Avoid the white foam. It breaks up into little pellets and doesn't sand well. 3M® makes a spray adhesive especially for foam that bonds almost instantly, so you can stack up layers of foam to get a mass of material very quickly.

Blue foam can be worked quickly with most woodworking machinery and hand tools. The board can cut cleanly with both a bandsaw and a tablesaw, sanded quickly with a disc sander (be sure to use a dust mask) or sculpted with a Surform® tool or a file.

A CUSHION THAT'S REALLY FOAM. High-density, white polyurethane foam shapes easily and is perfect to mimic upholstery in scale models.

Other materials are also useful for mock-ups: scrap wood for those times when cardboard just isn't strong enough, aluminum foil to simulate a mirror or metal parts, and construction paper or poster board bent, cut, or used like a veneer. Be creative.

When you build your mock-up, it's a good idea to make it easy to alter, so you can make changes without too much trouble. After all, you're really trying to see how the shape and proportion work, so a mock-up that's easy to adjust will be a lot more helpful than one with permanent joints. Be sure it is easy to disassemble, so the mock-up can be moved to a site or stored until completion of the real piece. Don't be tempted to toss the mock-up before the piece is completed. It will come in handy when you need to try out design changes that occur in mid-project.

A Scale Appearance Model

After the mock-up, I consider making an appearance model—a scale model that looks like the real piece only smaller. I make appearance models when I am designing a piece for production or if a one-of-a-kind piece is particularly sculptural, uses unusual construction techniques, or if the concept cannot be conveyed adequately with a drawing. A model gives a more realistic sense of the finished piece, especially if your drawing skills are weak; it makes a great presentation tool, and it can be used to create photos of a room setting when the job site isn't available for a mock-up.

A nice appearance model takes a day or two to build.

I make appearance models of furniture at one-eighth or one-quarter scale, according to the size of the project. It's best not to go overboard on detail, or the model begins to look too cute, like doll furniture. Small details also take time to do well and often don't tell you much. If they are really important, do the third type of model, a full-scale detail mock-up. More on that later.

Wood is the primary material on most of my appearance models. I used to mill my own small stock, but I found that it was time-consuming to cut the very thin stock that is necessary. And quite often, the quality was not as good as the store-bought model-making material. It can be tricky to mill small stock without having it explode in the planer or chip badly. Many hobby shops and architectural supply stores carry a good selection of basswood, cherry, and walnut. I avoid balsa because it doesn't cut cleanly. Many of the places that carry model-making supplies also sell ultra-thin plywood. I have seen three-layer sheets (1 ft. by 2 ft.) of ply as thin as ⅟₆₄ in.

When the project calls for a substance other than wood, I use a variety of materials. Blue foam is good for simulating the look of upholstery. There is a better quality,

white, high-density polyurethane foam available in sheets ¼ in. to 2 in. thick that is more expensive but holds details better and is more uniform (see the photo on p. 61). You can paint it with acrylic paint.

Acrylic sheet or rod can be used to simulate metal or glass. It can be bent with heat from a heat gun, torch, or in an oven and painted with a metallic paint. I have used pieces of acrylic sheet to simulate glass tabletops by painting the edges green (a light green marker is even easier).

Painted wood can be used to simulate other materials. For example, there are faux marble paint kits available in paint stores or art supply stores, so you can machine a tabletop in wood and then make it look like marble or granite. To make the patterns look right on scale models, you may have to alter your technique slightly. For instance, to get a smaller pattern that looks right, a tight-pored sponge, like a sea sponge, works best for marbling.

Don't overlook paper as a model-making material. When used like a veneer, it is quicker than paint and can simulate laminates and stone. Art or graphic supply stores carry paper in glossy or matte finishes, and the number of colors will surprise you. Ask for Pantone® paper. While you are in the graphics department, get a can of instant spray adhesive made just for paper.

And don't leave until you check out some markers, pencils, and press-on stripes and patterns. Architects and designers use these to simulate details; you can too. You can draw on inlays or drawer and door lines. A dot can simulate a knob, a horizontal line can suggest a wire pull, and markers can simulate aniline dyes. There are wood-colored markers, but you need to test the color to see if it approximates the real wood color.

Special tools help model making

Though the construction of scale models can be relatively quick, it requires some special tools and fixtures to make the machining of small parts safe and accurate. For example,

I made a small-parts crosscut jig for my radial-arm saw (see the bottom photo on the facing page). The jig helps block off the big gap in the fence that could swallow up small parts as they are being cut to length.

To deal with this gap problem on the tablesaw, I made a wooden throat plate with a narrow slot. I also can rip thin material on the tablesaw without having it slip under the bottom edge of the fence by using an easily installed facing for the fence that goes all the way down to the table surface. I always use push sticks; sometimes I use two, one in each hand. Featherboards are also good for keeping your fingers away from the cutting edges.

Joinery for models I often simplify the joinery on appearance models. I use butt joints when I can get away with it, but I also use thin dowels or wooden toothpicks for through-dowel joints when necessary. Dado joints are pretty easy with a router table and $\frac{1}{16}$-in. and $\frac{1}{8}$-in. straight bits. Make certain that the hole in the table is not so large that it creates a safety hazard when machining small parts. I use little De-Sta-Co clamps to make quick jigs to hold the small parts when I machine them on the router table.

Mortise-and-tenon joinery may seem a bit extreme, but occasionally, I find that it provides detailing important to the look of the finished piece. And it may help hold the model together. I drill out holes and clean out corners just like I do in full-scale mortise joints, but I use a shopmade $\frac{1}{16}$-in. chisel. I made the chisel by grinding the tang end of an old, dull file. The steel is hard enough to keep an edge.

One store-bought model-making tool that I find useful is the tiny brass bar clamp. The bar clamps are handy because they fit in small places. Other good clamping tools are clothespins, paper clips, tape, and rubber bands.

Scaled construction hints at real problems Although the tools are smaller, scale model making provides a good opportunity to think through the whole construction process on full-scale pieces. As I build the model, I imagine that I am doing everything in full scale, and based on that experience, I choose the best construction technique for the real piece. It is important to remember, however, that if a construction operation or detail is easy in scale, it may not be when it is full size and vice versa. For example, once I neglected to account for how difficult it would be to lift a glass top in and out of a frame repeatedly to get a perfect fit; on the model, it was easy to fit because the small piece of acrylic was so light. Conversely, some things can be awkward on a scale model because the access is tight or the parts are so small that clamping is difficult, but on the real thing, access may be a simple matter of reaching your arm inside of a cabinet or using a bar clamp.

Full-Scale Detail Mock-Up

Mies van der Rohe, the famous architect, once said, "God is in the details." So when I am working on a piece that has unusual edge or surface treatment, a unique pull, connection, or foot, I mock up just the detail. The full-scale detail mock-up lets you see your design in three dimensions. If you have already made a full-scale mock-up of the entire piece, then it's a good idea to attach this detail mock-up to it (see the top photo on the facing page). Work precisely on the detail mock-up so that you can work from it to build the real thing.

My material of choice is foam, both the blue and white types discussed earlier, because foam is so easy to work. When I use wood, I prefer something that can be worked easily, such as pine. Wood is the obvious choice if the detail is turned on the lathe or if it requires a texture that cannot be expressed in some other quickly worked material.

JAN ZAITLIN is an industrial designer and a furniture-maker in Albany, Calif.

As I build the model, I imagine that I am doing everything in full scale, and based on that experience, I choose the best construction technique for the real piece.

Photos Make Models Look Real

Scale models that are made with care can be photographed to look like full-size pieces, as shown in the photo at right. This is a great design and presentation tool.

Determine the Background

The easiest background is a sheet of paper large enough to fill the picture frame. Use any color paper as long as it isn't glossy. Bend the paper, don't crease it, so it sits on a tabletop and runs up a wall behind the table. For a more dramatic effect, use a roll of background paper, available in a variety of colors from professional photo supply stores. Tack one end to the wall, and put a table about 3 ft. away from the wall. Roll the paper onto the table, and set the roll on the floor. Place the model on the paper near the front of the table, and focus light there. The background fades into darkness, which contrasts with the lighted model.

Photos of the Piece on Site

To see what the piece will look like on site, I use three pieces of foam board taped together on the back side to form two walls and a floor large enough to house the model and fill the picture frame (see the photo below). To give a sense of scale, I use a few props. This can be as simple to do as drawing an outline of a door with a circle for a knob at the right height. When I was photographing a model of an audio-visual storage system, I drew a screen on a cardboard television set, which was just a rectangle of gray cardboard propped up from behind with a little cardboard triangle.

Figures Add Human Dimension

I find scale figures helpful, too. You can make a quick one by photocopying a figure from an architectural graphics book or a department store advertisement. Enlarge or reduce the figure until it is the right size. Use spray mount to fix the figure as a

MODELS LET YOU LOOK at the result in advance. This scale model of a conference table comes to life when photographed with a few props and an appropriate background. Cardboard or clear acrylic human figures add scale.

cutting guide to any rigid, thin material, like ⅛-in. acrylic. Then glue a small triangle to the back of the figure to make it stand on its own.

Photo Tips

In addition to a 35mm camera, I would suggest that you use a macro lens or a set of magnifying lenses, called close-up filters, which screw onto a lens to allow you to focus at much closer distances than standard lenses. A tripod and a cable shutter release allow you to snap a shot without wiggling the camera. Light stands can be fashioned with clamp-on shop lights and a chair for a stand. But daylight shooting is often quicker and can be just as effective. Just be sure that your film is matched to whatever lighting you choose. Any good photo supply store can give you advice on choosing the correct film.

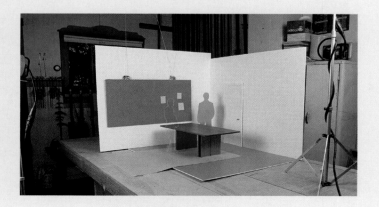

THREE PIECES OF FOAM BOARD can make a room—With the camera pulled back, the illusion is revealed. The backdrop is held up by string and tape. Simple shop-style clamp lights can substitute for the electronic flash shown here.

Organize Your Projects

ONCE YOU HAVE a clear vision of a woodworking project, either through concept sketches or from measuring an existing piece, the next step is to create a bridge between the idea and the actual construction. This means defining your vision on paper with working drawings, usually a three-view (orthographic) projection (see "Creating Working Drawings," pp. 47–52).

I use these drawings to generate a bill of materials, which functions both as an order sheet and as a data base from which to develop the cutting lists—one for solid stock and one for sheet stock, if any. These lists show the number, the size, and the detailing of every piece of wood that goes into the project. Sometimes I also make graphic representations of the cutting lists to help me determine the most efficient use of the stock. Last, I cross-check carefully from the drawing to the bill of materials to the cutting lists to make sure that they all agree.

Once you have accurate cutting lists in hand, you can begin the actual construction process by laying out the components. When all the parts are marked on the stock, it's clear sailing—no more knitted brow and clenched teeth. You can leave behind all that left-brain, analytical thinking and enjoy the process of cutting, shaping, and assembling the components.

Creating a Bill of Materials

To ensure that all the parts of a project will be accounted for in the bill of materials, and later in the cutting lists, create a referencing system. On the three-view drawing, label each component with a circled letter. You needn't bother to label separate identical components, such as four legs of an end table (as long as they're all made from the same material). To make organizing the bill saner, especially with large, complex projects, label the largest components first, working your way down to details such as moldings and drawer parts. Be sure to place material under the appropriate stock heading—solid or sheet—and add a notation for species if you're using more than one kind of wood.

As you list each item in the bill of materials, add a second circle around the letter on the drawing. When all the letters are double-circled, you'll have accounted for every component. Double-check by comparing the number of items on your bill of materials against a count of components shown in the drawing.

When listing widths and lengths of components on the bill of materials, be sure you've taken any joinery into account. It's easy to overlook the extra length you'll need for tenons or the width for tongues

BY JIM TOLPIN

FROM THREE-VIEW DRAWING to bill of materials to cutting list, step-by-step organization can all but eliminate measurement errors. By taking care of the calculations and accounting up front, you can concentrate on attaining accuracy and perfecting technique.

A POUNCE WHEEL IS USEFUL for transferring layout information either directly to the stock, if you only want one piece of that design, or onto template material, such as ⅛-in. lauan plywood or Masonite, if you want a more permanent record to reproduce the piece later.

Bill of Materials to Cutting Lists

Develop the cutting lists directly from the bill of materials, collating the components by function and then by dimension. Establish a heading for thickness first, and then create subsidiary columns for each width (see the photo on p. 65). Under the appropriate width, write in the length of each piece. If the components aren't simply square-sided (without profile), add a cross-sectional graphic next to the length. If there are a number of identical parts, make tick marks to the right of the length to indicate how many. Don't confuse yourself with numerals here. As with the bill of materials, list the largest pieces first, double-circle the letter symbol on the bill once you transfer it to the cutting list and double-check by comparing the number of components on your bill of materials and cutting list.

If I have a lot of components to cut out of sheet stock, I make a graphic cutting diagram (scaled drawings of 4x8 panels) on which I juggle the layout of the components to get the most out of each sheet. I account for sawkerfs, and I pay attention to grain by book-matching pairs of doors or cutting a bank of drawer faces from a single section of a sheet, for example. To make the panels easier to handle, I try to arrange the components so that the first cuts are full-length rips, giving me lighter stock to deal with when crosscutting.

when joining boards with tongues and grooves. If your three-view drawing does not specify the sizes of these joints, lay them out on a full-scale drawing. Unless you note otherwise, assume that the length of the components runs with the grain of the wood.

BENDING A BATTEN TO points along a curve is the best way to lay out long, gentle curves. For fair curves, use a square batten.

Laying Out on Solid Stock

With the cutting lists completed and double-checked against the bill of materials, you're ready to lay out the components on the boards. As you bring each previously thicknessed board to a leveled pair of sawhorses, set them down so that most defects face up. Mark the locations of any defects from the underside of the board onto the visible face with chalk. Always "waste" a minimum of an inch at each end of a board when squaring it, and take off more if splits are obvious.

Fig. 1: Drawing an Arc

1) Mark points A and B, where the arc leaves the stock, and draw a line indicating the height of the arc.

2) Swing compass or trammel from points A and B, both above the height of the arc and below the stock, on an extension board.

3) Draw a line through the points defined by the intersection of the compass or trammel beam swings. Point C is the apex of the arc.

Workpiece

Height of arc

A   B

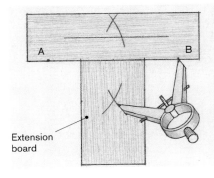

Extension board

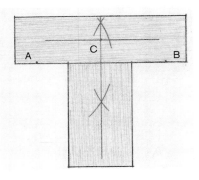

4) Repeat steps 2 and 3, except swing from B and C instead of A and B. Where this new line (perpendicular to the segment between B and C) intersects the line you drew in step 3 is the pivot point for the arc you wish to draw.

5) Set compass or trammel to the distance between D and A (or B). Swing arc through A, B, and C.

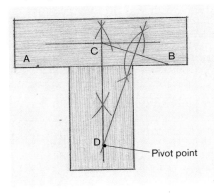

Pivot point

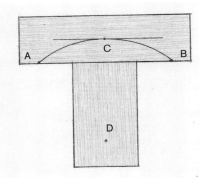

If the board rocks on the leveled sawhorses or bows significantly, it's probably best used for short components. Try to lay out components to make the most efficient use of a board. Work around knots and other defects, keeping an eye out for grain matches and striving for an overall pleasing look for the visible faces of a project. Finally, try to arrange the layout so the offcuts are long lengths; shorter, wider offcut pieces generally make less useful stock for future projects.

Use a piece of chalk or a timber crayon to mark out the pieces on the stock. Lay out pieces ½ in. long at this point and at least ³⁄₁₆ in. wide. It's easier to remove wood later than it is to add it back. Leave pieces even wider if you know the stock tends to curve as it's ripped. As you locate each component on the boards, pencil in a tick mark to the left of the length notation on the cutting list. When the tick marks on the left equal those on the right, all the pieces of this width and length have been accounted for.

Laying Out Sheet Stock

Panels are a lot easier to lay out than boards. Stock sizes are uniform, edges are straight, and except for occasional shipping damage, defects are negligible. If you're going to cut panels on a tablesaw and your rip fence and crosscut box are accurate and reliable, there's no need to transfer the layout from the graphic cutting diagram to the stock. Simply set the rip fence or stop on the crosscut box to the measurements on the cutting list, and make the cuts. Label each component along an edge with a marking pen, and put a second circle around the symbol denoting that component on the cutting diagram.

Joinery and Complex Shapes

Once you've cut out all the components, it's time to lay out for joinery, assembly positions, and for any shaped (non-rectilinear) components. I don't use measurements to do this, though, because for me, placing my faith in numbers at this stage is an invitation to disaster. Instead, I use a full-scale drawing. Then I either transfer it directly to my stock using a pounce wheel, a small, gear-like wheel designed for this purpose (see the top photo on p. 66) or I make a template. When using the pounce wheel, I follow the wheel with a light chalk dusting or with a pencil line to make the impressions left by the wheel more visible. If

there's a chance I'll want to make a piece again, I make a template; if I know a piece is a one-off, I just pounce onto the stock.

To transfer the shape of a complex or irregularly shaped component, such as a scalloped table apron, I always use a full-scale template. To make the template, I tape vellum tracing paper (available at art supply stores) over the area of the full-scale drawing containing the component and trace its shape with a #2½ pencil. Then I pounce the pattern onto a piece of ⅛-in. lauan plywood. I bandsaw this pattern to within 1⁄16 in. of the line, and then use rasps, files, and sandpaper to finish the job. I can use this plywood pattern to reproduce the component indefinitely. A set of templates representing each component contains all the information I need to reproduce a project; it's a durable, accurate and highly efficient way to keep this information at hand.

Laying Out a Curve with a Batten

To draw a fair curve, whether on a full-scale drawing, a template, or directly on the stock, use a batten held to a series of points along the curve (see the bottom photo on p. 66). I make battens from clear, close-grained wood. Old-growth fir or spruce is ideal, though nearly any knot-free, straight-grained stock will do. Cut the batten square to keep the curve fair—from ⅛ in. for tight bends to ¾ in. for long, gentle curves.

To determine a few points along the curve, draw a 1-in. grid pattern over the area of the full-scale drawing containing the curve. Draw the grid on actual stock or on template stock. Determine where the curve intersects the grid lines on the drawing, and transfer those points to the grid on the wood. When working from a scaled drawing, draw the grid on the drawing at the same scale, lay out the curve at scale, and transfer it to the wood.

Set finish nails at those points, and bend the batten stock to touch each nail. Prevent

LAYING OUT ROUND CORNERS is easy with marking gauge and compass. Set both for the same radius, mark intersecting lines with the gauge, and you have a pivot point.

AN EFFECTIVE AND CHEAP centering scribe can be made from a piece of scrapwood, two dowels, and a drywall screw, as the author demonstrates above.

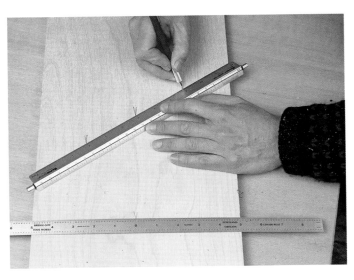

CENTERING RULES AND REGULAR RULES are both useful for locating centers. They can also be used for establishing regular intervals across a board's width.

the stick from breaking by applying the bending force from near the end of the batten rather than just beyond the points you've marked. Where necessary, sandwich the stick between two nails to hold it in place. At the ends of the curve where the batten leaves the board, add extension boards to which you can fasten the free ends of the batten. Don't let the protruding ends just run straight. That would cause the curve on the board to go out of fair between the points marked on the stock.

Before drawing in the curve, eyeball it. You can readily see if it's a sweet, fair curve. Don't hesitate to let your eye overrule a marked point to make it fair.

Drawing an Arc with a Compass

If a curve is nothing more than an arc (a portion of a circle), you can use a compass or a trammel beam to draw it. The only trick is finding the center of the circle—the pivot point for the compass or the beam. It's not difficult to do, but it's not exactly intuitive either, hearkening back to high school geometry, which may not be all that fresh in your mind anymore. Figure 1 on p. 67.

Laying Out Rounded Corners

Unofficially, I draw in rounded corners by reaching into my pocket, taking out a fistful of change and using a coin as a round template: A penny produces a ⅜-in. radius arc; a quarter produces about a ½-in. arc and a half dollar gives you a ⅝-in. arc. For larger radii, I've even rummaged through my finish supplies for cans with a radius close to what I wanted.

Officially, and when I'm out of change or fed up with using out-of-round cans that leave a ring of old paint or oil on the wood, I use a marking gauge and compass to draw in a rounded corner quickly and accurately. I set the marking gauge to the radius I desire and run the gauge along each edge of the wood to the corner. At the intersection of the lines, I place the pivot point of my compass, which I've set to the same radius as the marking gauge, and I draw in the rounded corner.

Laying Out Equal Divisions

Sometimes, when laying out a piece of furniture, you need to divide a board into parts of equal width, whether halves, thirds, or more parts. Centerlines are often needed to locate joint cut lines or assembly positions. Multiple divisions are needed to locate the parts of certain joints, such as dovetails. Components that are to be located evenly between two points, such as chair slats, must be laid out so they end up with equal spacings between them. The process can seem complicated, but with certain layout tools and just a little bit of arithmetic (the first and only time I'll burden you with number crunching), these tasks can be made a lot easier.

The simplest way to find a centerline across the width of a board is to use a centering rule, a rule that reads both to the right and to the left of a 0 at the center of the straightedge (see the top right photo on p. 70). To find a center point, you need only position the rule so that the same number appears over each edge, and the 0 will indicate the center point.

A standard rule can be used to locate any number of equal divisions across a width. Let's say that you want to divide an 11-in. board into four equal pieces. To do this, lay the rule on the board with the 0 point over an edge. Then set the 12 (a multiple of 4) on the other edge of the board (see the top right photo on p. 70). In most cases, you'll have to angle the rule to do this. Now just mark your division lines (here, 3, 6, and 9), and then extend or transfer them, using a marking gauge (or a combination square if the end of your board is square).

To draw centerlines over the length of a piece of stock, I made a simple centering marking gauge, consisting of two dowels, a little block of scrap and a common drywall screw (see the top left photo on p. 70). When using the gauge, it's important to keep the dowels tightly against both sides of the stock. A nice feature of this type of gauge is that the centerline remains true even if the stock changes in width along its length.

Now for the math. To determine the centerlines of a number of components spaced evenly between two points, it's necessary to know how many components you want to fit in the space and how wide the space is. Let's assume you want to space three chair slats evenly between chair posts that are 16½ in. apart (see Figure 2 on the facing page). Add the width of one of the slats (3½ in. in this case) to the width of the space between the posts (16½ in.) for a total of 20 in., and then divide this sum by the total number of spaces (4) between slats and posts: 20 in./4 = 5 in. Now mark the centerlines of the outside slats at 5 in. less half the width of a slat (1¾ in.), or 3¼ in. from the post. Mark the centerline of the middle slat at 5 in. from the centerlines of the two outside slats.

JIM TOLPIN is a writer and woodworker in Port Townsend, Wash.

Fig. 2: Spacing Components Evenly between Two Points

If components are centered on equal division lines, spacing won't be equal.

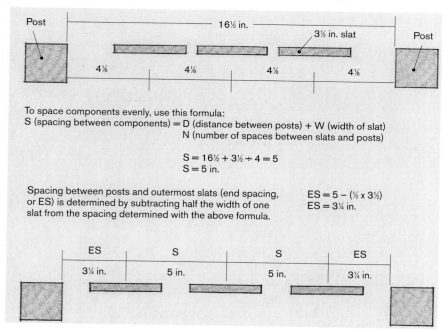

To space components evenly, use this formula:
S (spacing between components) = D (distance between posts) + W (width of slat)
                                              N (number of spaces between slats and posts)

$$S = 16½ + 3½ ÷ 4 = 5$$
$$S = 5 \text{ in.}$$

Spacing between posts and outermost slats (end spacing, or ES) is determined by subtracting half the width of one slat from the spacing determined with the above formula.

$$ES = 5 - (½ × 3½)$$
$$ES = 3¼ \text{ in.}$$

A Drafting Table for Shop or Home

BY CAMERON RUSSELL

THE DRAFTING ROOM at the college where I teach furniture making had long been a sore spot with me. The tables we used were industrial-type library tables, not designed for drawing. The students who used them were far from comfortable. For hours at a time, they hunched over a flat surface that was at the wrong height. It made drafting a pain.

To solve that problem, I designed and built the prototype shown in the top photo on p. 73. After working out the bugs in the design, I realized that this would be a good beginner's project for the woodworking class. By the time the projects were finished, we had refitted the drafting room at the school, and the students were a lot more comfortable.

The construction process is simple, and the hardware we used is readily available from hardware stores or mail-order supply houses. The knockdown design makes it easy to disassemble the table for storage or moving. The torsion-box top is rigid and dead flat, yet light and portable.

The key hardware components holding the table together are four threaded rods that fit within metal pipes. The nuts and washers on the ends of the threaded rods pull the leg assemblies firmly together while the rigid lengths of pipe keep the two sides apart. This combination of tension and resistance to compressive forces stiffens the structure. The smooth cylindrical surface of the metal pipe also provides an ideal pivot pin for the tilting top.

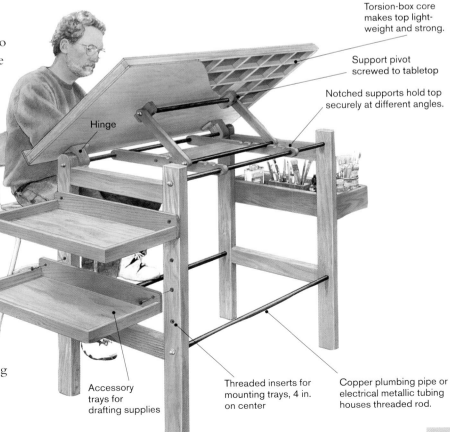

Torsion-box core makes top lightweight and strong.

Support pivot screwed to tabletop

Notched supports hold top securely at different angles.

Hinge

Accessory trays for drafting supplies

Threaded inserts for mounting trays, 4 in. on center

Copper plumbing pipe or electrical metallic tubing houses threaded rod.

Torsion-Box: Light but Strong

The design for the top guarantees that it will be lightweight, dead flat, and strong. The outside skins of ¼-in. plywood are glued to the narrow surfaces of an internal wood frame, and the considerable overall surface area makes a healthy bond. As with any face-to-face gluing of wood, this construction process offers a lot of resistance to twisting forces, making the panel very rigid for its size and weight.

I built this tabletop 24 in. wide by 42 in. long, but the lower structure could easily handle a top up to 30 in. wide by 60 in. long. If you plan to fit a drafting-arm machine or a parallel straightedge to your table, take that size into account when you determine the length of your top.

The internal framework of the top's core consists of ribs of lumber ½ in. wide by ¾ in. thick, as shown in the drawings and photos on p. 74. It's a good idea to add a few wider blocks to receive the fasteners that secure the pivoting top to the lower frame. The extra size gives you a little more leeway for mounting the hardware.

Mill all the lumber for the ribs at the same time to ensure they're all the same size. Also, accurately marking the locations of intersections where ribs are joined together is important. Apply a small spot of glue to each joint, and drive a staple to span the seam. Use a small-gauge staple and gun. Once one side of the frame is complete, flip it and staple the other side.

Gluing the plywood skins to the core frame requires a lot of pressure. A large veneer press is ideal, but if you don't have one, you might ask someone at a local cabinet shop to glue up the skin for you. You can do it yourself by sandwiching the top between sheets of plywood weighted down with bags of cement or boxes of nails. In any case, mark the hinged edge before adding the outside skins—you'll avoid trouble later

A Good and Simple Design

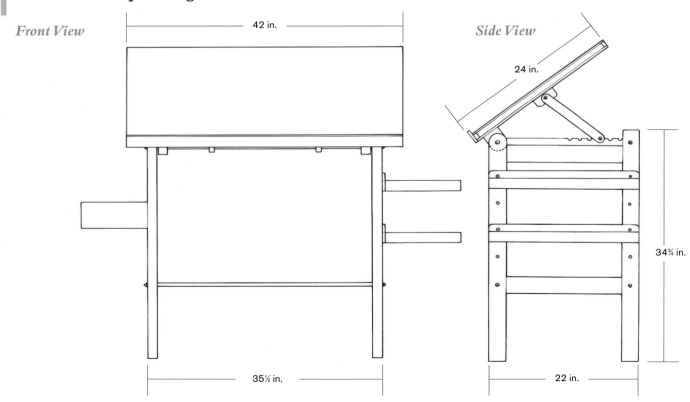

Front View

42 in.

35½ in.

Side View

24 in.

34¾ in.

22 in.

A Knockdown Drafting Table

Built with common materials and knock-down hardware, this table is inexpensive and easy to make. Movable hinged supports make it possible to adjust the top to different angles. Accessory trays mounted on the sides provide plenty of storage space for drafting materials.

when you want to install threaded inserts for the wood-hinge mounts.

Legs and Notched Support Rails

Each side of the table is made with a front and rear leg joined by two rails, as shown in the drawings on the facing page. We used mortise-and-tenon joints to connect legs and rails, but either dowels or biscuits also could be used.

The size of the table calls for standard lengths of 36-in. threaded rod. The pipe can be either thin-walled, ½-in. EMT (electrical metallic tubing) or ½-in. copper plumbing pipe. The copper is much more expensive, but it can be polished and clear coated for a visually pleasing finish. If you use the EMT,

you might want to dress it up a bit with primer and paint.

When drilling holes for the pipes in the legs (and in the prop pieces for the underside of the top), drill the counterbored pipe holes first. You can use the center point left by that hole to line up the bit for the smaller hole that the threaded rod passes through. Depending on the type of pipe you choose, the diameter of the hole may or may not be a standard size. It's critical for the overall sturdiness of the table that the pipes fit snugly within the counterbored holes with no slop.

A ⅝-in.-dia. hole should be right for the ½-in. copper plumbing pipe. The outside diameter of ½-in. EMT is between ¹¹⁄₁₆ in. and ¾ in. The best method I know for getting a

Building the Torsion Box

The core framework of pine is lightweight and rigid. The six frame pieces that are wider receive threaded inserts to hold the top to the hinged support pieces.

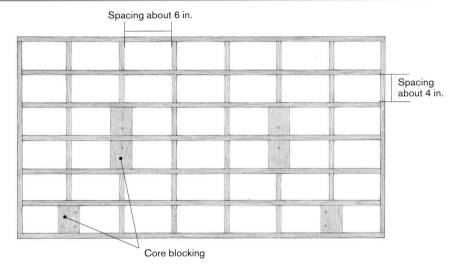

Spacing about 6 in.

Spacing about 4 in.

Core blocking

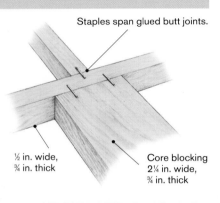

Staples span glued butt joints.

½ in. wide, ¾ in. thick

Core blocking 2¼ in. wide, ¾ in. thick

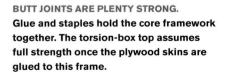

BUTT JOINTS ARE PLENTY STRONG.
Glue and staples hold the core framework together. The torsion-box top assumes full strength once the plywood skins are glued to this frame.

Construction Details

These drawings show the important details of parts that connect the top to the lower frame. For rigidity, the holes for the metal pipe should have flat bottoms and furnish a snug fit. If you use a spade bit (right), you may have to grind it down.

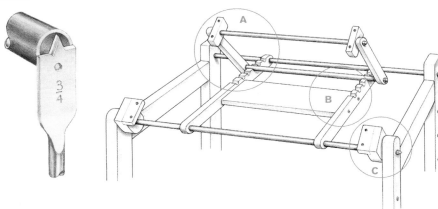

A. Section through Top Prop

Threaded insert

Core blocking

Pivot support piece

Connector bolt

11⅜ in.

Top prop piece

Acorn nut with washer

Threaded rod

½ in.

Metal pipe

Ends cut at 1¹⁄₁₆ in. radius.

Counterbored hole for pipe is not drilled all the way through.

1⅜ in.

C. Section through Top Hinge Mount

Threaded insert

Core blocking

Threaded rod

Metal pipe

Hinge

Acorn nut with washer

1½ in.

Leg

1½ in.

B. Section through Notched Supports

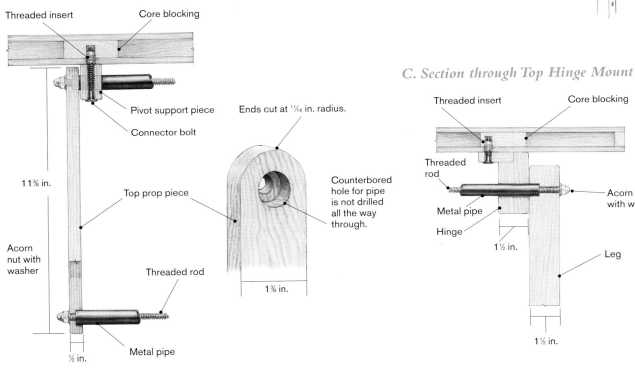

Cross dowel and connector bolts secure notched supports to rail.

¾ in. radius

1½ in.

⁵⁄₁₆ in. radius

1½ in.

19½ in.

21 in.

ACCESSORY TRAYS ARE ADJUSTABLE. They are fastened with connector bolts to threaded inserts mounted in the legs. The author's design calls for two shallow trays and one deep one.

hinge blocks mounted to the underside of the top, be sure to drill the hole large enough to allow free movement. Sand and finish all the wood parts before assembly.

Assembling All the Parts

Once you've fabricated and finished all the pieces, putting them all together is a cinch. Start with the legs and notched support-rail assembly. It's important to remember to slip the hinge-block pieces over the pipe as you do this, so the hinge blocks are in place when you want to secure the top later. The only tools you'll need to set up this table (or take it apart) are a box wrench, a ratchet for the threaded rods with acorn nuts, and an Allen wrench for the connector bolts.

The small blocks of wood that allow the top to pivot and to be supported at different angles are bolted through into threaded inserts set into the underside of the top. For applications like this, where I thought parts would have to be taken apart and put back together many times, I used threaded inserts and bolts.

If you plan to assemble the table and leave it set up, you could certainly substitute regular wood screws for some of this hardware. Keep in mind, though, that ready-to-assemble hardware makes adjustments easy when aligning the moving parts of the tilting and supporting pieces.

I also installed threaded inserts on the outsides of the legs for rearranging or adding accessory trays for drafting equipment (see the photo above). You could customize your own table to handle other specific accessories, such as a paper-roll holder or a T-square rack.

CAMERON RUSSELL teaches furniture making at Camosun College in Victoria, B.C., Canada.

snug fit for the EMT is to file or grind down a ¾-in. spade bit until it makes a hole into which the pipe fits just right. Don't forget to mark the bit, so you don't get it mixed up with your standard-sized bits.

The other wood parts are easy to cut, drill, and shape. Half-round holes in the notched supports (see the drawing on p. 75) can be drilled by clamping two pieces together, edge to edge, and using the joint line as the centerline. With any part that must revolve around the metal pipe, like the

Doors
Make the
Difference

BY CHRISTIAN
BECKSVOORT

THE MOST OBVIOUS FEATURE of many wall cabinets, kitchen cabinets or even freestanding cabinets is the doors. By changing the style of the door, you can subtly or significantly alter the appearance of the cabinet, as I found on a recent job when I ended up making five different doors for the same carcase.

I wanted to design a simple wall cabinet that mounts on a hidden hanger (see the sidebar on p. 80) and that would function in a variety of settings. I started with a basic box for the carcase, as shown in the drawing on p. 81, with the idea of making the door the main attraction.

I carefully selected quartersawn stock for the frame material for this door (and all subsequent doors) to minimize movement. For the single, flat and flush panel, I used a wildly flame-figured cherry board given to me by a friend. Once oiled and polished, the figure seemed to leap off the panel, as

DOORS CAN SIGNIFICANTLY AFFECT the appearance of a cabinet. A simple frame and flat panel are perfect for showing off the wildly flame-figured panel of this door.

shown in the photo on p. 77. The simple frame-and-panel construction was the perfect showcase for this magnificent piece of wood.

As I stood admiring my handiwork, I began to wonder, what if . . . ? One idea led to another, and soon I was at work on door number two. For this door, I decided to divide it horizontally with a center rail, yielding two stacked, flat-flush panels. The results were okay, but compared to the incredible figure in the first door, door number two seemed rather plain. It needed something to set it apart. After a little midnight inspiration, I took a carving gouge to the panels and textured their front faces, as shown in the left photo below. This was a simple but

time-consuming process that required some care and a sharp gouge, especially around the edges to avoid tearout. The oiled, carved facets gave the panels a nice three-dimensional look, but I couldn't help wondering if the door might not look better divided vertically.

Thus I began door number three. This door has a vertical center stile and two thin, flat, book-matched panels. I framed the panels with 7/32-in.-wide quarter round moldings to add some detailing and to create an entirely different look, as shown in the right photo below. An alternative method would be to shape or rout the stiles and molding into the rails. But this requires

HAND-CARVED PANELS CRE-ATE an interesting textural effect in an otherwise plain door. Dividing the door horizontally makes the cabinet look shorter and wider.

A VERTICAL CENTER STILE and thin, recessed panels give this cabinet a tall, narrow appearance. Quarter-round moldings are an easily added detail.

more complicated joinery to assemble the door frames.

Door number four was a combination of doors two and three. Door four had vertical panels as in door three, but the panels were flat, flush and carved as in door two. I really liked the tall, thin, clean lines of this door, as shown in the left photo below. To accentuate the look, I did away with the knob and routed a finger pull on the edge of the door frame. This was my favorite door so far, but what if...?

To give the piece a bit more versatility, I decided to make one last door. Door number five is glass paneled to serve as a display cabinet. A single piece of glass set in the mortised-and-tenoned frame provides an unobstructed view of the cabinet's contents, as shown in the right photo below. A small, quartersawn, horizontal panel at the bottom of the door covers three drawers. Carved pulls recessed in drawer fronts maximize interior drawer space.

At this point, I decided to stop making doors. Although I hadn't yet made the standard raised-panel or gotten into complex carved lattices, end-grain or stained-glass panels, I now had four more carcases to build for my door collection. One has to quit somewhere.

CHRISTIAN BECKSVOORT is a contributing editor to *Fine Woodworking* and a custom furniture maker in New Gloucester, Maine.

CARVED, FLUSH PANELS SEPARATED by a vertical stile add texture to the long, lean look. This combination of styles became the author's favorite door.

A FRAME-AND-GLASS-PANEL door turns a storage cabinet into a display cabinet. Glass provides a view of the contents, and three drawers hide behind the solid lower panel.

Hidden Cabinet Hangers

A French cleat makes hanging wall cabinets a breeze. The cleats are easily screwed to the wall and cabinet; then it's a simple matter to press the cabinet against the wall and slide it down so that the cabinet's cleat interlocks with the wall-hung cleat. Recessing the cabinet back an extra ½ in. completely hides the hanging system.

Normally, the wall cleat spans at least two studs and is anchored in a couple of places. Because my cabinet is only 14 in. wide, I was able to screw into only one stud. A single screw into the usual narrow wall cleat would allow the cabinet to swivel on the wall but might not offer sufficient support for the cabinet and its contents.

My solution was to make a T-cleat, as shown in the drawing at right. The bottom of the T is tenoned into the wall cleat and extends down the wall another 17 in., providing plenty of extra space for screwing the cleat to a single stud. Be sure to level the cleat when screwing it to the wall.

After screwing the top cleat to the cabinet-back frame, the cabinet is ready to drop into place on the wall cleat. As a safety feature, I also add a small brass screw through the panel back into the hanger.

Single Stud, French Cleat Hanger

Rip at 45° after vertical support is tenoned into cleat stock to create cabinet-back cleat and wall cleat.

Cabinet-back cleat

2¼

2¼

13

Pin

Wall cleat

½

Flat-head wood screws (#10 x 3) secure cleat to wall.

Tenon, ¼ x 1½ x 7, glued only at center

Vertical support, ½ x 8 x 17

Flat-head brass wood screw (#6 x 1) screwed though cabinet back and into hanger keeps cabinet in position on cleat.

ADJUSTABLE SHELVES AND DRAWERS with carved pulls enhance the simple features of the dovetailed carcase. Also shown is the routed finger pull used on the carved, flush panel door.

Five Doors to Dress Up the Basic Box

Door One

Door Two

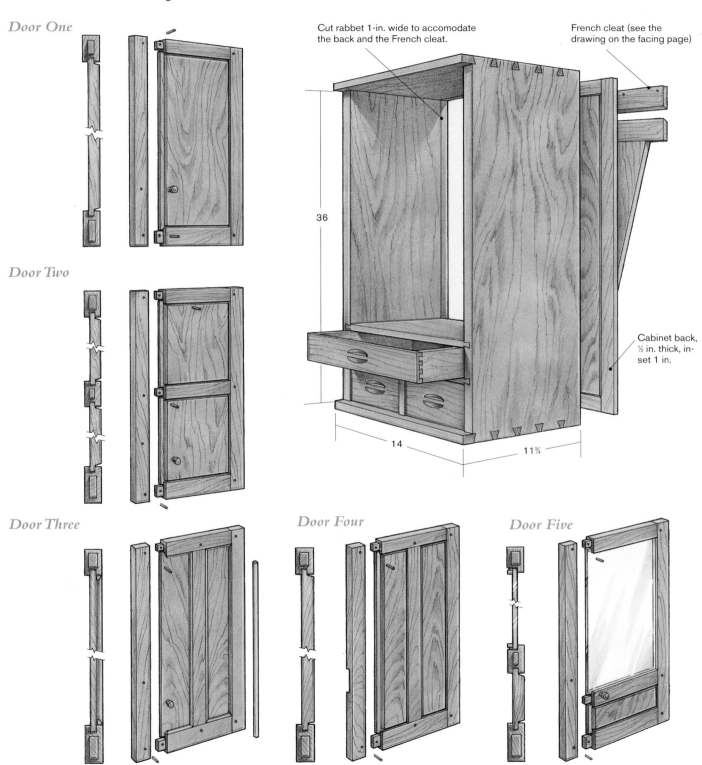

Cut rabbet 1-in. wide to accomodate the back and the French cleat.

French cleat (see the drawing on the facing page)

36

Cabinet back, ½ in. thick, in-set 1 in.

14

11¾

Door Three

Door Four

Door Five

Joining Legs to Aprons

BY GARRETT HACK

THE LIFE OF A TABLE is often not easy. Legs get kicked; the table gets pushed and pulled across uneven floors, leaned against and sometimes even sat upon. To make matters worse, the very nature of wood adds to the stress. As the tabletop shrinks and swells with seasonal changes, the movement works against the integrity of the table's structure. Where is all this stress felt? It's the leg-to-apron joint that holds a table together and gives it rigidity. When that joint fails, the table falls apart.

Leg-to-apron joints must withstand three different kinds of stress. One is shear—a vertical load directly above a joint, such as when someone sits on the corner of a table. Leaning heavily on the top of a table midpoint above the apron causes the joints to undergo a bending stress trying to lever

them apart. Shoving the table sideways or bumping against a leg gives the joints a mixture of twisting forces. Also, as a tabletop that is fastened too tightly to the apron expands or shrinks, it can try to twist the joints. The best defense against these stresses is a well-designed, tight-fitting mortise-and-tenon joint that locks apron to leg. The mortise and tenon is not only a good joint for tables, but the same principles also apply to designing joints for cabinet doors and chairs.

Size the Tenon

When deciding on the sizes of joinery components, the key is to attain a workable balance. Too large a mortise, and you risk weakening the leg; too skimpy a tenon, and you lose glue and mechanical strength. The ideal joint would have a large tenon with

Where Tenons Meet

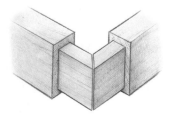

Miter them, but skip the glue on the very ends. The author does not bother to glue the end grain of the miters, reasoning that the bond is unreliable.

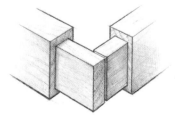

Butt them together if you have tenons of unequal width.

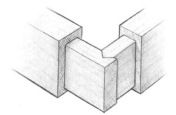

Bird's-mouth joints often are found in Asian furniture. This design offers additional strength because the tenons interlock.

lots of glue surface, it would be the full height of the apron to best resist twisting, and the mortise would be cut from the center of the width of the leg for maximum strength. But it's not just the sizes of the mortise and tenon that you have to balance: The shoulders on both sides of the tenon must be substantial enough to do their work. They butt against the leg and resist bending and twisting forces trying to lever apart the joint. A good rule of thumb is to size the tenon thickness a little more than one-third the thickness of the apron.

While the one-third rule is a good general guide to follow, sometimes it's better to make exceptions. If I'm building a table out of butternut or a similar softwood, with aprons only ¾ in. thick, I make the tenons at least ⁵⁄₁₆ in., maybe even ⅜ in. thick. Any smaller and a sharp bump to the leg might snap the tenon right off. Because you rarely see the thickness of an apron, one good design strategy is to make it thicker—⅞ in. or 1 in. will provide larger, stronger shoulders.

Maximize Tenon Length

Two other aspects of the tenon affect the joint strength. One is the amount of long-grain glue surface on the cheeks of the tenon; the other is the length of the tenon, which is affected by where the mortise is cut on the leg. Naturally, a longer tenon has more glue surface and provides more mechanical strength to the joint. As a general rule, the longer the tenon, the better, assuming the leg can accommodate it. A tenon length that's three to four times its thickness is quite adequate. When laying out the size and placement of tenons, a full-scale, top-view drawing will help you understand the orientation and relationship of all of the parts.

One engineering principle states that the stress on any part is least along the centerline or neutral axis. A centered mortise or tenon is stronger because it has all of that wood on both sides bolstering it. For this reason, I prefer to have a shoulder on both

sides of a tenon (rather than one side only) to better resist bending stresses from either direction. Even a small shoulder will cover any bruised edges on the mortise that result from cutting the joint.

A centered mortise might be ideal, but the farther to the outside of the leg you position a mortise, the longer the respective tenon will be. Too far out and the cheek of the mortise is more vulnerable to splitting under stress. Deciding on the exact placement is a judgment call that varies with each project. I have butted tenons together inside the leg, but doing so makes one tenon shorter than the other. Butting tenons together works when joining aprons of unequal width, where the wider tenon can be the shorter one because it has extra glue surface. I've also cut half of each tenon

THE SIZE AND LOCATION OF **mortise-and-tenon joints affect their strength.**

A Sturdy
Leg-to-Apron Joint

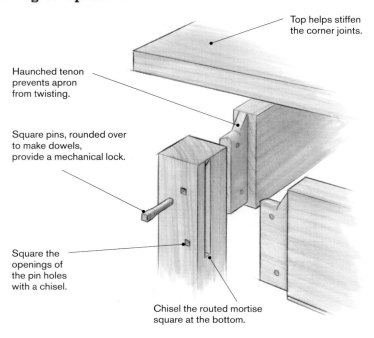

Top helps stiffen the corner joints.

Haunched tenon prevents apron from twisting.

Square pins, rounded over to make dowels, provide a mechanical lock.

Square the openings of the pin holes with a chisel.

Chisel the routed mortise square at the bottom.

Top View

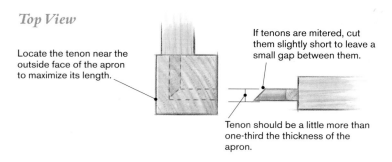

Locate the tenon near the outside face of the apron to maximize its length.

If tenons are mitered, cut them slightly short to leave a small gap between them.

Tenon should be a little more than one-third the thickness of the apron.

Side View

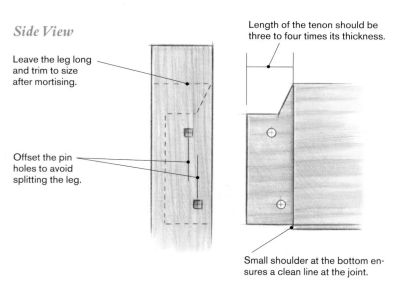

Leave the leg long and trim to size after mortising.

Offset the pin holes to avoid splitting the leg.

Length of the tenon should be three to four times its thickness.

Small shoulder at the bottom ensures a clean line at the joint.

long and the other half short and locked one tenon into another with a bird's-mouth cut as Chinese furniture makers sometimes do. But I prefer to miter the tenons within the joint without actually joining them. This is easy to do, and it can add 15% to 20% more glue surface and length to the tenons. If I must incorporate drawers into an apron, the size of the rail usually calls for a completely different tenon design (see the sidebar on p. 88).

Shorten the Tenon Height with a Haunch

A tenon the full height of the apron affords lots of glue surface and strength against bending and twisting forces. But there's a trade-off: A full-height mortise weakens the leg, especially if there are two mortises at the corner of the leg. With the top of the mortise open, any serious stress on the apron can more easily split the top of the leg. So the strength of such a joint relies almost entirely on the glue bond because the mechanical strength is compromised.

A simple solution, and one I prefer, is to shorten the tenon considerably for the top ¾ in. to 1 in. or so and cut an angled haunch. With this design detail, what little glue surface you lose is balanced against having a much stronger mortise.

I cut the haunch on the tenon by hand with a dovetail saw and then clean it up with a chisel. For speed and accuracy, I lay a wooden template on the tenon to mark out the haunch and use another one made as the mirror image of that pattern to size the mortise at the haunch end. To cut the mortise for the haunch, I first mark out the sides aligned with the mortise with a mortise gauge, chop the waste, and refine it using the template and a chisel. Because I cut many of my mortises with a router bit, I keep the top of the mortise below the haunch round for a small measure of added strength. Also, a small ⅛-in. shoulder at the bottom of the apron tenon will hide any

Begin by Routing the Mortise

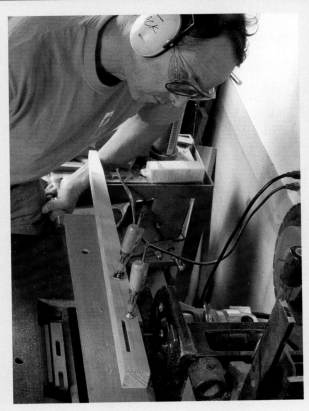

1 Routers are quick and accurate. Although his mortises often require additional handwork, Hack cuts most of them with a machine he made from scrap parts. It has a router mounted horizontally to a sliding table that can be adjusted in three dimensions.

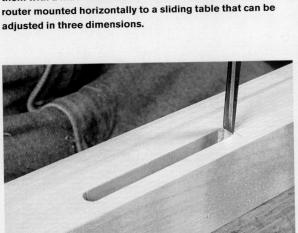

2 Cut the bottom square. Use chisels to clean out the bottom corners of each mortise as an index to seat the tenons later on.

3 Scribe lines for the haunch. A marking gauge extends the lines of the existing mortise that indicate where to cut the angled haunch.

4 Chisel the haunch by hand. There is no other practical way to cut the slope for this shape. Hack leaves the table legs long to keep them from splitting along the top edge while he chisels the haunch.

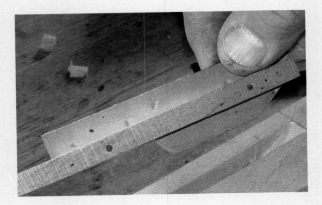

5 Check the results using a small shopmade template. The template makes it easy to check your progress as you cut the angled mortise.

Fit the Tenon
to the Mortise

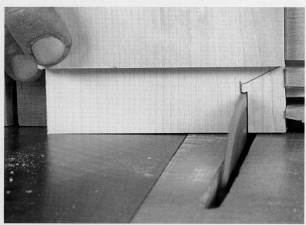

TENONS ON THE TABLESAW. With the workpiece firmly clamped against this tenoning jig, the tablesaw can cut tenons cleanly and accurately.

TRIM TENONS TO SIZE and shape. A matching template made to the negative shape of the one used to check mortises shows where to cut the angled haunch on the tenons. The first cut is made with a stop block on the miter gauge.

THIS HANDWORK IS FAST and accurate enough. A dovetail saw makes quick work of trimming the angled haunch and mitering the ends of the tenons.

Glue and Pin
the Joint

YOU DON'T NEED a lot of glue. With snugly fitting mortise-and-tenon joints, a thin layer of yellow glue spread evenly is all you need for a good bond.

PINS ARE AN INSURANCE policy. Small hardwood pins will hold the joint tightly, even if the glue fails. Hack leaves the outside end of the pin square and holds it with a wrench as he hammers it home.

small inaccuracies in cutting the mortise, and it allows for vertical alignment when the table is assembled.

Adjust the Fit and Use Glue Sparingly

The best design and the strongest glue won't overcome a joint with carelessly fit shoulders or a sloppy fit between tenon and mortise. Even when I cut these joints with accurate machine setups, I still often find it necessary to improve the fit with a few passes of a shoulder plane or a chisel. I want the shoulders to fit tightly over their entire surface and the tenon to slide into place with a minimum of force for a good glue bond.

Part of the long-term strength of the joint is the snugness of the fit, or what I call its mechanical strength. Glue adds strength, but how long does a glue bond last? By its very nature a mortise-and-tenon joint has wood fibers running cross-grain to one another, which weakens the bond. Flexible modern glues can accommodate some of this movement.

Before gluing, I always dry-fit and clamp the parts together to discover any problems that may arise while there's still time to solve them. To ease assembly, I chamfer the ends of each tenon. Glue-ups can be stressful, but it is worth taking care to place the glue so as to avoid drips and oozing joints

Unique Solutions for Different Design Problems

Not all aprons call for a single haunched tenon mortised into the leg. The problems presented by some leg-to-apron joints require uncommon solutions. One example is an apron that incorporates drawers into the design, such as those you'd find on a desk or some kitchen tables.

Aprons with drawers often have a narrow rail under the drawers that joins into the leg, and such rails have tenons that can't be any higher than the height of the rail, nor probably any longer than the other tenons joining into the leg. Still, these tenons are doing quite a bit of structural work. The solution is to make double tenons parallel to one another, which doubles the glue surface and provides good resistance to twisting and bending forces (see the top drawing at right).

Extrawide aprons offer another example of design problems that require different solutions (see the bottom drawing at right). Wood movement over such a wide apron is, of course, a consideration. But more than that, another real concern is that a long mortise can weaken the leg. The long sides of the mortise can flex easily, and the apron-to-leg joint loses vital mechanical strength. The solution is simply two mortises with a groove for a stub tenon between them and an angled haunch at the top. The two mortises still have plenty of glue surface and lock the apron along its full height. If wood movement is a concern, glue only the top part of the tenon, then pin the lower part with elongated holes, as you would on a breadboard end, so that the apron can move slightly. Also, cut the bottom mortise a little long to accommodate the anticipated movement.

Two Tenons Are Better than One

Narrow rails under drawers need beefier tenons. Doubling them up maximizes the strength you can get from such a small piece of wood.

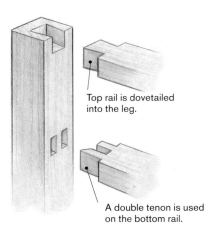

Top rail is dovetailed into the leg.

A double tenon is used on the bottom rail.

Wide Aprons Need a Break

A mortise longer than 4 in. or so can threaten the structural integrity of a leg. A break in the middle for a haunched tenon alleviates that problem but still keeps the apron from twisting.

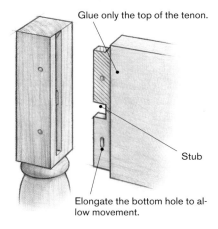

Glue only the top of the tenon.

Stub

Elongate the bottom hole to allow movement.

that would be a headache to clean up later. With a thin stick about half the width of an ice-cream stick, I apply a light amount of glue into the mortise and on both tenon cheeks. The flat edge of the stick is perfect to squeeze out the glue in a thin, even layer. Another trick that works well is to cut a light chamfer around the mortise to contain any squeeze-out. Ideally, the joint should slip together under light clamping pressure.

For large tables and for peace of mind, I often pin the leg-to-apron joints. I use a hard, straight-grained wood such as rosewood, ebony or maple for the pins. A contrasting wood can add a pleasing visual detail, and two small pins are stronger than one large one. Most often, I drill holes for the pins after gluing and drive them in either from the outside or inside of the leg, depending on whether or not I want them to show.

GARRETT HACK is a professional furniture maker and a contributing editor to *Fine Woodworking* magazine.

Graduated Drawers

BY CHRISTIAN
BECKSVOORT

THE SHAKERS WERE AMONG the primary proponents (and practitioners) of graduated drawers, although there are lots of cases—Chippendale, Federal and Queen Anne—that have graduated drawers. Under the dictum "a place for everything and everything in its place," the Shakers built drawers to house specific items. There is no reason for a drawer that will hold cassette tapes to be as deep as one that holds CDs, or for your underwear drawer to be as high as your sweater drawer.

Also, I never build solid wood drawers much more than 9 in. high. Because of seasonal wood movement, anything higher will leave too wide a gap in midwinter (even with overlay drawers), and the drawer could bind in summer.

Another consideration is overall proportion. Small drawers in desks or in a collector's cabinet may graduate in only ¼-in. to ⅜-in. increments. In bureaus used for clothing, on the other hand, the drawers can be graduated in ¾-in. or 1-in. increments. If

A Case with an Even Number of Drawers

The formulas for the example here—a four-drawer chest with 1-in. graduations—can be used for any chest with an even number of drawers.

To get the usable drawer height, subtract the dimensions of the top (1½ in.), base (5¼ in.), and drawer dividers (3 x ¾ in. = 2¼ in.) from the chest's total height (36 in.):

$$36 - (1½ + 5¼ + 2¼) = 27$$

To find the average drawer height, divide the usable drawer height (27 in.) by the number of drawers (4):

$$27 ÷ 4 = 6¾$$

To find the height of the drawer below the middle divider, add one-half the graduation increment— 1/2 in.–to the average drawer height (6¾ in.):

$$½ + 6¾ = 7¼$$

Add 1 in. to the drawer height below and subtract 1 in. from the two above.

36 in.

1½ in.

5¼ in.

6¼ in.

7¼ in.

8¼ in.

5¼ in.

Three drawer dividers at ¾ in.: 2¼ in.

A Case with an Odd Number of Drawers

A case with an odd number of drawers has a middle drawer with an equal number of drawers above and below it. The method of determining the average drawer height is the same as for a case with an even number of drawers. The formulas for the example here—a seven-drawer chest with 1-in. graduations—can be used for any chest with an odd number of drawers.

To get the usable drawer height, subtract the dimensions of the top (5¼ in.), base (6½ in.) and drawer dividers (6 x ¾ in. = 4¼ in.) from the chest's total height (59⅛ in.):
59⅛ − (5¼ + 6½ + 4½) = 42⅞

To find the average drawer height, divide the usable drawer height (42⅞) by the number of drawers (7):
42⅞ ÷ 7 = 6⅛

For the drawers below the middle drawer, increase the drawer heights in 1-in. increments. For the drawers above the middle drawer, decrease the drawer heights in 1-in. increments.

you are a stickler for detail, you may also want to consider graduating the size of the knobs or drawer pulls as well.

Find the Usable Drawer Height, then Figure the Average Drawer Height

Once you know the height of the case and the number of drawers in the case, laying out graduated drawers is straightforward. To get the available drawer space, subtract from the total height the dimensions of the top, bottom and all of the dividers. The number of dividers in a case will always be one less than the number of drawers: e.g., a five-drawer case will have four dividers. Dividing the available drawer space by the number of drawers will give you the average drawer height. Regardless of whether you're building a case with an odd number or even number of drawers, the average drawer height is the most important dimension.

If you have an odd number of drawers, the middle drawer will be equal to the average drawer height. For the drawers above, simply subtract the amount by which you want the drawers to get smaller—the graduation interval—and add this amount to the drawers below the middle one.

When figuring drawer graduations for a case with an even number of drawers, you still need to find the amount of available drawer space and calculate the average drawer height. However, there will be no average-height drawer in the case when you are through; the average drawer height is just the starting point in your calculations. Determine an average drawer height, then add or subtract one-half the graduation increment to or from that average height to get started. Then proceed by full graduations.

Always remember that you have some flexibility. If needed, you can add a fraction of an inch to the top molding or remove a fraction of an inch from the base to make the numbers work in a simple way (making your life a lot easier) without compromising the chest. You probably can't change the dimensions of your dividers, though, which have to be a specific size if they are to fit into dovetails or dadoes cut with a standard router bit.

The illustrations shown are examples of how to graduate the drawers for a case with an even number of drawers and for one with an odd number of drawers. Here's an important thing to keep in mind: You can graduate drawers by any increment—1 in., 2 in., 3 in., even fractional inches—as long as you subtract the increment from the drawers above the average-height drawer and add the increment to the same number of drawers below the average-height drawer. The formulas can be used for any number of drawers, from the smallest case with three drawers to a floor-to-ceiling built-in with 16

CHRISTIAN BECKSVOORT is a contributing editor to *Fine Woodworking* magazine.

5¼ in.

3⅛ in.

4⅛ in.

5⅛ in.

6⅛ in.

7⅛ in.

8⅛ in.

9⅛ in.

6½ in.

59⅛ in.

Six drawer dividers at ¾ in. = 4½ in.

Exposing Your Back Side

BY CHRISTIAN BECKSVOORT

THE BACK PANEL of a lot of case goods is an afterthought, quickly screwed into place before pushing the carcase against a wall where the back is never seen again. But for freestanding pieces or glass-front display cabinets, the back can become the center of attention. When a cabinet back has to play an up-front role, there are a variety of traditional techniques for installing backs that work well. I'll discuss how these techniques have been adapted to contemporary pieces and present an overview of my method of installing a frame-and-panel back.

On display or hidden away, a back serves some important functions. It adds strength and racking resistance, which is most important for open cases and those with adjustable shelves. On closed carcases, the back keeps the contents in and dust, dirt and foreign objects out. When the back is exposed, it should be visually appealing. And, finally, a back that is square, will automatically square the carcase when it's installed.

Board Backs

Traditionally, narrow cabinets often had single board backs. Most often, they were set into rabbets in the sides and top, as shown in Figure 1. Nailed into place, the back provided strength and racking resistance while still

A RAISED PANEL CAPTURED in grooves in the carcase effectively seals the cabinet against dust and light. Although attractive, this type of back doesn't strengthen the carcase as much as a frame glued into a rabbet.

Fig. 1: Back Installation

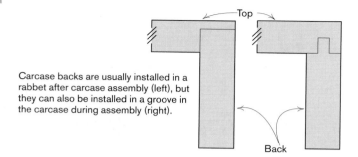

Carcase backs are usually installed in a rabbet after carcase assembly (left), but they can also be installed in a groove in the carcase during assembly (right).

Fig. 2: Back Panels from Individual Boards

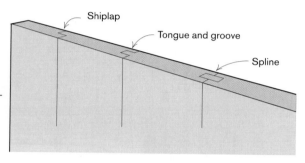

A variety of interlocking joints can be used when making up a back panel from individual boards.

Fig. 3: Mortised-and-Tenoned Back Frame

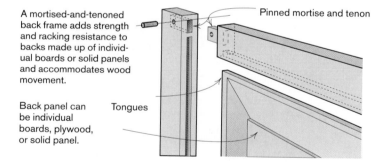

A mortised-and-tenoned back frame adds strength and racking resistance to backs made up of individual boards or solid panels and accommodates wood movement.

Back panel can be individual boards, plywood, or solid panel.

Fig. 4: Back Panel Options

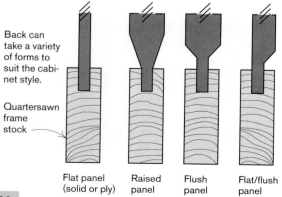

Back can take a variety of forms to suit the cabinet style.

Quartersawn frame stock

Flat panel (solid or ply)   Raised panel   Flush panel   Flat/flush panel

allowing the wood to move. Rarely, single board backs were set into grooves in the carcase before assembly. A variation of this type of back, that includes two boards separated by a center stile, is shown in the photo on p. 91. Done properly, this method provided a dust-proof, virtually air-tight closure that was also visually attractive. But because space must be left between the carcase and the board to allow for expansion and contraction, this method doesn't provide as much racking resistance for the case.

On wider cabinets, individual boards were joined in a variety of ways, such as shiplap, tongue-and-groove or spline joints (see Figure 2). The shiplap is easy to make but has a major drawback: If adjacent boards bow in opposite directions, the joint opens, allowing in dust, dirt and light. Nailing shiplapped boards to a fixed center shelf can overcome this problem, as shown in the photo on the facing page. The tongue-and-groove joint solves the problem of warping boards by interlocking the tongue of one board to the groove of its adjacent board. A minor drawback to both the tongue and groove and the shiplap is that they consume ⅜ in. to ½ in. of the board's width for the overlap. When making a 4-ft.- or 5-ft.-wide walnut back, this loss to the overlap can prove costly. The spline joint, which is easier to cut than either the shiplap or the tongue and groove, eliminates the waste by butt-joining boards with thin strips that can be ripped from waste.

Whichever method is used, the boards must be allowed to move. They cannot be glued into place but, instead, must be nailed into the rabbet. However, individually nailed boards don't offer much racking resistance and shouldn't be used on large, empty cabinets, especially those without integral face frames.

Plywood Backs

Plywood is flat, thin, attractive, has negligible movement and comes in 4x8 sheets. Because it doesn't move, plywood can be glued into rabbets to provide the ultimate in racking resistance. Yet plywood, too, has minor drawbacks. Unless grain direction is irrelevant, it can't be used on pieces wider than 4 ft., and it comes only in a limited variety of species. Also, plywood's thin veneer faces make it difficult to repair nicks, dents and scratches.

Frame-and-Panel Backs

This brings me to my favorite back, the frame and panel, shown in the photo on p. 94. Built just like a door with stiles, rails and panels, it has all the qualities I require for a back: strength and racking resistance, air and dust-tightness, solid-wood construction of the same species as the rest of the cabinet and a pleasing appearance that enhances the overall look of the cabinet. Small cases usually get a single panel frame. Tall cases can have two or three stacked panels. Low, wide pieces may require several side-by-side panels. And large pieces like wardrobes may have stacked and side-by-side panels (see the photo on p. 94).

A frame-and-panel back can include some features of other back styles. For instance, individual boards can be set into a mortised-and-tenoned frame (see the photo at right). This maintains the look of the traditional, individual-board back while adding to its strength. Another alternative is to use ¼-in.-thick plywood for the panels. Because the plywood is recessed into the frame, the panel is protected from most nicks and scratches.

But I prefer to use solid-wood panels in frames. This gives me the most flexibility regarding the species of wood used as well as the style of the panel. Like doors, backs can have a variety of panel styles to suit the style of the cabinet, as shown in Figure 4.

Although my first choice is usually a flush panel, I've used several different panel styles. Other options include ¼-in.-thick, solid flat panels, a variety of raised-panel styles or combination panels with a flat face on the interior and a raised panel face on

the exterior. Non-wood materials, such as stained or translucent glass, melamine, slate or composition panels covered with leather or velvet, also can be used for panels.

Building a Frame

I like to use ⅜-in.-thick stock for the frames in all but the smallest cases. This thickness represents a good compromise between strength and weight. Frames ¾ in. thick add too much weight, especially on large cases, and ½-in.-thick frames yield weak mortise-and-tenon joints. I use narrow, quartersawn stock for the frame members to

SHIPLAPPING **Framing shiplapped boards is stronger than nailing the boards directly into the back rabbet. Nailing through the boards into a fixed shelf further strengthens the beautiful back on this cabinet built by Ron Layport of Pittsburgh, Pa.**

A FRAME-AND-PANEL back with flush panels is built like a door with stiles, rails and panels and is glued into a rabbet in the carcase. It provides racking resistance and keeps dust and air out.

but the panels are free to float in the frame grooves. A loose wood panel can be anchored to prevent it from rattling in the groove. Center the panel in its frame, and then drive a 20-gauge brad through the frame and the panel tongue, centered at both the top and bottom of the panel.

Installing the Back Panel

Before installing the assembled back frame and panel into its rabbet in the completed carcase, I trim the panel assembly square to fit snugly into the rabbet, using the tablesaw, jointer and a block plane. The carcase rabbet should be 1/32 in. deeper than the thickness of the back. To make it easier to slide the back frame into the rabbet, I chamfer the edge along the inside face of the frame with the block plane. I also mark the locations of all the carcase's fixed dividers and shelves and the bottom, so I can nail through the back frame into these components to further strengthen the carcase. Just prior to installation, I sand the back panel to 320-grit on the inside face and ease all the sharp edges.

Finally, I glue the back into place, spreading glue thinly on both faces of the rabbet as well as the edge of the back. After forcing the back into the rabbet, I clamp top to bottom first and then side to side. There should be no gaps between the back frame and the rabbet. Because the back has been squared, it will automatically correct a minor out-of-square carcase as the back is clamped into place. When the glue is dry, I remove the clamps, drill holes at the previously marked dividers, shelves and bottom and nail the back with 4d finishing nails. I countersink the nails about 1/4 in. and then plug the hole with small, 1/8-in.-sq. pegs of the same species wood as the carcase. I trim the end-grain plugs flush, plane the carcase flush to the back, sand the entire back to 320-grit and, again, ease all frame and panel edges.

CHRISTIAN BECKSVOORT is a contributing editor to *Fine Woodworking* magazine.

reduce wood movement. Quartersawn stock moves roughly half as much as plain-sawn stock. By keeping the frame members 1¼ in. to 1¾ in. wide, the overall movement is limited to under ¾₄ in. (for quartersawn cherry) no matter how wide the back. This amount of movement is easily handled by the compression of the wood fibers and will not push apart the carcase or break the rabbet joint.

If the bottom rail of the frame is not captured in a rabbet, as shown in the photo above, like all other secondary stiles and rails, can be made as wide as desired. A wider bottom rail allows larger mortise-and-tenon joints and makes a stronger back frame. The mortises and tenons are glued and pinned,

Making Dining Tables That Work

BY PETER TISCHLER

"MAKE FURNITURE THAT people can be comfortable living with," said Sam Maloof, the noted chairmaker. This same guiding principle is at the heart of the furniture I build. Optimum comfort certainly applies to chairs, and the same holds true for dining tables. When building a dining table, I start by finding out how the owner likes to dine and where the table is going. I use this information to come up with rough sketches and scale models, which convey material and proportions better than drawings. Then I measure everything—people, dining room, rugs, existing furniture, and china—so I can translate dimensions to drawings and occasional mock-ups.

Design Is Always a Compromise

How a dining table relates to its users is just as important as how it relates to its surroundings. The best tables are the ones that make tiny compromises. For example, when building a table for a family with children, the durability of the finish on the tabletop outweighs the need of the finish to be authentic to the table's style period. Fortu-

nately, there are some simple guidelines that will help with design decisions.

Seating The first step is to determine the number of people to be seated, so you can figure the table size that will fit them comfortably. If the owner entertains regularly, you'll want to make a table with an expanding top that doesn't require a complicated leaf system or a forest of legs. General rules (for example, the commonly given 24 in. of elbow room per person) may have

SHAPING REFINES A TABLE'S design. The author first uses models, measurements and full-scale drawings to work out a dining-table design. Plywood templates (foreground) help execute that design. But even so, subtle shaping in the shop makes the table more inviting to the touch and to the eye.

IT TAKES MORE THAN a measuring tape for good table design. The author uses small models, full-size chair and sideboard mock-ups, full-scale drawings and templates.

Measure Everything before You Cut Anything

After you've figured out the seating and overall table size, take out a tape measure, sit at a comfortable dining table, and think about the relationships of sitter to chair to table.

Then start taking real-life dimensions. With the biggest sitter in a relaxed, seated position, measure the distance between his or her elbows and knees. Measure knee heights, and add a little extra to establish the bottom of the apron height. Measure how far forward the person likes to put his or her feet. Measure dinner plates, serving platters, and the room where the table is going. Exact dimensions aren't as important as how they all relate.

Models Show Table Proportions and Styles

Most styles of furniture offer variations for dining tables, such as top shapes, woods to use, and options for bases. It's worth looking at lots of examples of the period you're working in because you may have to do some hybrid designing to come up with a table that matches a sideboard or china hutch. Similarly, if you're making a contemporary table, it's useful to know the tastes of your client because you're likely to borrow the lines or elements of his or her favorite furniture pieces. Here's where models can help.

When I build quarter-scale table models, I make several variations to help the customer visualize differences in proportions and materials. I use various woods to show what color, figure, and grain patterns will look like in the room. Alternative shapes for the top, such as free-form edges and book-matched halves, are another example of what models can depict. Models can also present a variety of base forms, which show how much room there will be under the top and how stable the footprint will be. The following are the four most common base types I use.

to be increased or decreased depending on the the type of table, the space needed for the chairs, or how else the table might be used. Figure 1 shows a typical table plan for seating six people.

Basic dining dimensions I've found that the most comfortable height of a dining table is between 28 in. and 28½ in., which is a bit lower than what the textbooks say. But for a family, that height is more informal and makes the sitters feel relaxed. The height, of course, depends on the chairs and whether the table has an apron that will limit leg clearance (see Figure 2 on p. 98).

The width and shape of a dining table's top also affect seating arrangement. Most chairs are 20 in. wide or so, but you will need better than 24 in. of place-setting width for most people and even more if you're dealing with squirming teenagers. For the minimum overall width of the table, I use 36 in. A table much over 40 in. wide will lose any feeling of intimacy between eaters on opposite sides. An oval top offers more side seating than a rectangular top of similar square footage. (It's easier to squeeze two more people in at the ends of an oval when company comes over). But because square and round tables take up less space, they often fit better in small dining areas.

Single pedestal In terms of stability and looks, the mahogany model (the first one in the photo below) shows the relative proportions a single-pedestal table should have. An oval top resting on a single-pedestal base will allow for extra sitters. Because this type of table has a central column, it makes sense to have an even number of people on each side (an odd number can cramp the person sitting in the middle). Single pedestals also lend themselves well to a round top, but there is a size limit that the pedestal will support. I limit round tops to 54 in. dia., unless the undercarriage is quite heavy. A rectangular top on a pedestal shouldn't be much over 72 in. long.

Double pedestal A double-pedestal table (the second model in the photo below) will fit an odd number of sitters per side staggered around the columns. The model shows how a free-form top, here in wormy red maple, looks over a walnut base. The top's slightly asymmetrical shape, which widens in places, actually offers extra knee space where the curved vertical members are. The two pedestals spread out the center of gravity, so the table can be quite long. Double-pedestal tables are good for expansion (using draw leaves) because the place settings will be in the right spots.

Trestle Trestle tables (see the third model in the photo below) are great for accommodating many people because there are lots of expandable-top options. Even with-

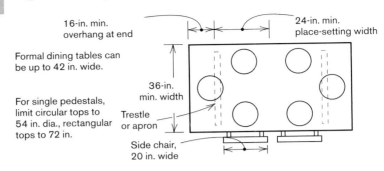

Fig. 1: Dining Dimension Guidelines

16-in. min. overhang at end

24-in. min. place-setting width

Formal dining tables can be up to 42 in. wide.

36-in. min. width

For single pedestals, limit circular tops to 54 in. dia., rectangular tops to 72 in.

Trestle or apron

Side chair, 20 in. wide

out leaves, a trestle table can be long because the length mainly depends on the strength of the stretcher and how far the top boards can span. In the case of the trestle model, the book-matched cherry top has butterfly keys joining two large boards, similar to classic George Nakashima tables. The model also shows that the base uprights are shaped inward at knee level to accommodate sitters at the ends of each side.

There are two major drawbacks of a trestle table: First, it requires lots of overhang (compared with a leg-and-rail table) at each end to give enough room for end sitters. To allow for this, pull a chair up to the edge of a dining table, and measure how far in the ends are. I generally allow 16 in. as a minimum amount of overhang all around the tabletop. Second, the trestle's feet interfere with people seated at the ends of each side.

QUARTER-SCALE MODELS SHOW table options—From the left, the model bases are single pedestal, double pedestal, trestle, and leg and rail. Models also present wood choices.

DESIGNING FOR FAMILY NEEDS The author had the family in mind when he designed this table to seat six comfortably, with room for a high chair. He used end leaves to allow plenty of elbow and leg room without dividing or disrupting the figure in the tabletop's center.

Fig. 2: Seating Clearances for Dining

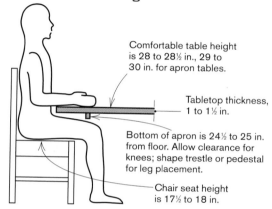

Comfortable table height is 28 to 28½ in., 29 to 30 in. for apron tables.

Tabletop thickness, 1 to 1½ in.

Bottom of apron is 24½ to 25 in. from floor. Allow clearance for knees; shape trestle or pedestal for leg placement.

Chair seat height is 17½ to 18 in.

Leg and rail Leg-and-rail tables, such as the fourth model in the photo on p. 97, can be strong, as well as quick and economical to build. But because a table's legs can take up much of the sitter's leg room, I give each sitter at least 28 in. of width for comfort because about 3 in. is lost around each post. Or a leg-and-apron table can be fitted with a bow-sided top, like the model, and the legs spread out to the corners to provide more seating room. I build leg-and-rail tables slightly higher—about 29 in.—to allow enough leg clearance because the apron will take up some height. To do this, determine the bottom of the apron height by measuring the largest sitter in a chair. Chairs are typically 17½ to 18 in. high at the seat. Allowing 6 to 7 in. for the thighs to go under the top, the bottom of the apron should usually be 24½ to 25 in. above the floor (see Figure 2).

The Importance of Scale Drawings and Materials

Proportions are such an important part of overall design. I've found that one-quarter scale drawings and models bring up the design issues and questions that I need to present to the customer. But to work out final construction details and to produce templates, I usually make full-scale drawings. I then use the templates to shape the parts (see the photo on p. 95).

There are benefits to using solid wood for the whole table, including the top. For me, the durability, variation in grain, and smooth transition of top to edge make solid-wood tops worth the effort. Though veneered tops may be stable and show consistent pattern and color, there are ways of achieving similar results in solid wood.

For stability, I use only well-seasoned stock. To keep the boards flat, I rough-mill in several sessions over two weeks to acclimate the wood to my shop. The best way I've found to keep consistent grain and figure patterns is by using the widest boards available. Wide boards are usually much easier to match than narrow ones.

For color continuity, I like the logs that are to be cut into tabletop stock to be sawn clear through. If this isn't practical, select boards from the same lot, and buy all your wood at the same time. Then when gluing up the top, go for the best grain match rather than trying to orient all the end grain a certain way.

Changes in top thickness as small as ¹⁄₁₆ in. can have a dramatic effect on how we perceive the table as a whole. My tops vary from 1 to 1½ in. thick. I allow extra thickness for planing the wood a few times before matching up the boards for glue-up. Longer boards will likely be cupped or twisted, so give yourself enough wood rather than under-sizing the top's thickness just to get it flat. When connecting the top to its base, allow for seasonal movement by using screws in slotted holes or cabinetmaker's buttons.

PETER TISCHLER is a North Bennet Street School graduate who runs a chairmaking and cabinetmaking shop in Caldwell, N.J.

Large-Case Construction Strategies

BY BRUCE COHEN

TACKLING BIG JOBS like my nine-drawer dresser used to be a nightmare. It has well over 100 parts and even more joints, but through the years, I've developed a few strategies that make the process a smooth and enjoyable one. I limit the number of details I have to keep in mind and break the process into easily manageable steps. With my tactics, I'm able to get the most out of my time, techniques, and materials. I also get a little more sleep.

I use quick but accurate drawings and cut lists to make sure that my projects are well organized even before I mill the first board. I dimension all the parts at once and cut my simplified joinery with only a few machine setups. Parts are always neatly stacked, clearly marked, and easily found. I first build small sections that are easy to handle and then bring them together in a final sturdy case. Assembly and glue-up becomes a rewarding and almost leisurely task.

Drawings and Cut Lists Help to Keep You Sane

Shop drawings are the only way I know to keep the details of a large case under control (see the left photo above). I first use the drawings to figure out the dimensions of each part, and then a final drawing helps me compile cut lists (see the top photo on p. 100). During milling and construction, I refer to the drawings and the cut lists constantly. To do otherwise with so many parts to keep track of would introduce errors and would risk endless confusion.

I reduce the potential for much confusion by making many details common to every case I make. These include the stock thicknesses, the tenon lengths, and the

99

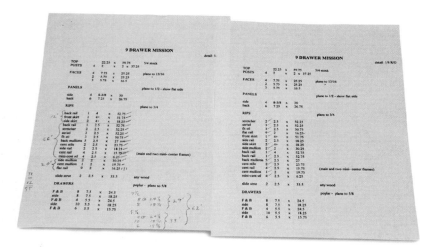

QUICK DRAWINGS AND CUT LISTS **save time and countless mistakes. Drawings and cut lists are used to double-check every stage of the construction process. Easy-to-read drawings show everything unique to the project (top photo on p. 99). Cut lists tell the dimensions of every piece even before the first board is milled.**

panel thicknesses. I keep these details in my head so I don't clutter my shop drawings with them. Only what's unique to the piece gets put in the drawings.

I always draw an isometric view of the front and one side, an elevation of the back, and a top view. Often I'll add views of selected internal frames, just to make sure I keep them straight. I like to keep all drawings on a single sheet attached to a clipboard so that they're easy to check while I work.

Once I have a shop drawing, I can calculate the dimensions of each piece. I then make two cut lists. One is organized around each section of the case (sides, back, internal frames). This list tells me what goes where and what joints to cut on which pieces. The other list is organized around the dimensions of the pieces—their length, width, and thickness before any tenons, dadoes, grooves, or moldings are cut. I list these pieces in descending order by size.

Each list is valuable at different parts of the milling and construction process. When dimensioning stock, I have the second list close at hand because I don't need to know where the pieces go, just how many pieces I need of any one width and length. Then when I cut the joints, I move to the first list. It tells me which part needs a tenon and which needs a mortise. When I've finished the drawings and both lists, I recalculate every dimension to catch omissions or errors. By investing two or three hours in the planning stages of each project, I have saved myself a lot of time and trouble over the years.

IT ONLY TAKES A FEW **machine setups to cut all the dado-and-tenon joints in a case. A single dado creates both mortises and panel slots. After tenon shoulders are cut on the tablesaw, a double blade is used to cut both cheeks in a single pass.**

NEAT PILES KEEP EVERYTHING in check. With all the parts in an organized pile, it's easy to spot a mistake at a glance. Write the purpose, location, and orientation on each part, somewhere that won't show and won't be sanded off.

Fast Ways to Dimension Stock Accurately

The larger the project, the greater the potential for small errors to accumulate into big problems. A ½₂ in. off here and a ¹⁄₁₆ in. off there can result in the case not fitting together during final assembly. Consequently, you need to be very accurate with dimensions, squareness, and flatness.

To reduce the chance for confusion, I make all frame stock ¾ in. thick and all panels ½ in. thick. The only exceptions are the corner posts, which are 2 sq. in. Fewer dimensions give fewer opportunities for error. I dimension all stock at once. The advantage of this approach is that I don't have to recreate exact machine settings to cut matching stock at a later time. Starting from the second cut list, I find the total linear footage of each width, adding some for waste and test pieces.

While I'm dimensioning stock (and cutting joinery), I keep similar parts in neat stacks (see the photos above). Organized this way, they serve as a visual checklist. If I see one that is odd, I can make sure that there is a good reason. With this system, I have caught many errors while there was still time to fix them easily.

When each piece is dimensioned, I label it according to its purpose and location in the finished case. If the orientation of the piece is important, I note it as well. This

helps tremendously during glue-up when I'm in a hurry and don't want to spend the time figuring out whether I have the right piece in hand.

Simplified Dado-and-Tenon Joinery Saves Confusion and Time

Perhaps the most time-consuming part of large-case construction is the joinery. When each joint needs unique fitting, the work quickly becomes overwhelming. I solve this problem by limiting the joints I use to two very simple types and cutting each type all at once. I use either a dado-and-tenon joint or dowels. My doweling technique is conventional, but the dado-and-tenon joint I use is a considerable time-saver.

Instead of cutting a mortise to receive the tenon and a slot for the panel, I cut one ½-in.-deep and ¼-in.-wide dado to serve as both. I glue the tenons into the dadoes during assembly, but I leave the panels dry. A single dado cut on the edge of a board takes only a few seconds, yielding two mortises and a panel slot. Chopping deep mortises to receive tenons and then plowing dadoes to receive panels would take considerably longer. Because the dadoes are perfectly even in width, fitting the joints is only a matter of making sure the tenons are the right width. For a strong glue joint between the dado and tenon, the parts should go together with moderate hand pressure but be reasonably difficult to pull apart. If you dry-fit two pieces together and pick up one, the joint should stay tight.

I use the dado-and-tenon joint for almost all the framework in the case. The only exception is where the stretchers meet the front posts: There I use a ¾-in.-wide and ¼-in.-deep dado with dowels. I use a shaper to cut the dadoes, though a router or a tablesaw with a dado blade could do the work just as well.

The fastest way I know to cut accurate tenons is on the tablesaw. The shoulders come first. I feed the piece over the blade

with a miter gauge, using the fence to determine the width of the cut. I leave the blade low so that it doesn't cut into the cheek of the tenon and make it weak.

To cut the cheeks, I use a cast-iron Delta® tenoning jig and a double-blade setup in the tablesaw (see the bottom photo on p. 100). However, I don't use the ¼-in. Delta spacer between the blades because it's exactly ¼ in. thick. To cut a ¼-in. tenon with double blades requires a thicker spacer to compensate for tooth set. I had a machine shop make a custom spacer to cut tenons that match the ¼-in. dadoes perfectly (two-thousandths of an inch will affect the fit from too tight to too loose). This setup still needs to be shimmed for the exact fit, the same way you shim a dado gang. But with this setup, I can produce tight, reliable joints throughout the piece.

Breaking Down the Assembly Process into Manageable Parts

It is not possible to assemble a nine-drawer dresser in one fell swoop. It can also be very difficult to assemble one piece by piece. My solution is to divide the case into a number of smaller frames, which I assemble first (see the photo at left). The frames include the two sides, the back, and six internal frames. All sections are flat and easy to assemble. Afterward, assembling the frames into the complete case is just as easy.

I always dry-fit each section to check the fit. I take this opportunity to make witness marks to indicate where parts go together. When I glue the parts together, the lines will guide me. If the dry-fit is clean, I take the subsection apart and assemble it again with glue. I use prepared hide glue for several reasons. I like it for its long open time, making one-man glue-ups simply hurried and not panicked. Also, the parts are easy to disassemble when repairs are needed in the future.

IT'S FAR EASIER to assemble a large carcase in sections. Dry-fitting every part of a case ensures that glue-up won't present any surprises.

I've found that a small jig makes glue application less hectic. I drill a few ⁵⁄₁₆-in. holes into a scrap of wood. I fill most of the holes with the glue I'll need for the assembly and leave a few of them dry to hold the glue brush when I'm not using it. This way, I don't have to squeeze glue out of the bottle each time I need a little more.

After I clamp up the frames, I check three things. First I check the diagonals. Then I check the flatness of the frames. If the diagonals are not within ¹⁄₁₆ in., adjust the clamps until they are. If the frames are not within this tolerance, final assembly will be far more difficult and may result in a parallelogram-shaped dresser.

Preparing for a Calm but Quick Glue-Up

I find that the climactic final assembly of a large case is the most satisfying moment. It's when all the parts come together and start to look like something. But it's not the moment to rush. The time taken to dry-fit the assembled frames is always well spent. If the case is twisted, you'll know before drying glue has you under the gun. I use undersized dowels for the dry-fit, so I can get them back out for glue-up with full-sized dowels.

The key to a civilized glue-up of a large case is having everything ready and at hand. I place all the clamps I'll need within reach and get the glue ready. I make sure that I have a mallet to persuade unwilling parts.

Work I have put into the parts previously will come to fruition. If all of the frames are square, the case will be square. You do need to check the diagonals across the face. But don't chase your tail checking the squareness of each opening. There's no way to adjust them at this point. If all of the parts are labeled, it will be easy to figure out where they go. And if you use hide glue, you can take your time during glue-up to get it right.

The combination of these strategies will make it possible to move through the building process at a calmer pace and still finish a large case in less time.

BRUCE COHEN builds custom furniture in Boulder, Colo.

Designing a Chest of Drawers

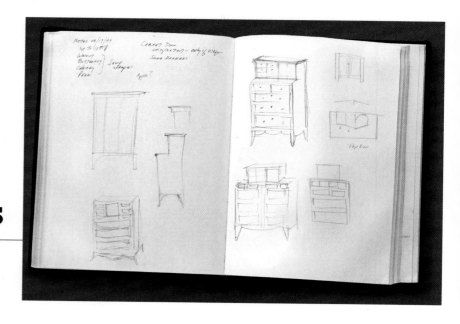

BY GARRETT HACK

THE CHEST FORM has been around at least 3,000 years, so it's hard to imagine designing something original today. I don't even pretend to. Instead, I freely borrow from this wealth of past ideas. Generations of craftsmen before me have played with chests in every way imaginable. They have refined everything from the sensuous sweep of certain curves to the basics of drawer joinery and case construction. Chests of drawers—from simple country chests to sophisticated highboys—are rich with ideas and lessons.

For me, originality comes not from trying to invent some new form or detail, but from some fresh and intriguing combination of ideas I've picked up along the way. I've been building and studying chests for years, and I've learned that knowledge builds on knowledge; you have to learn certain basics—about both design and construction—before you can understand more complex ideas. I can look at all sorts of furniture and absorb ideas, but only by actually building a piece that incorporates those ideas do they become part of my design vocabulary. And more importantly, I begin to understand new directions in which I can push those ideas next time. When thinking about a design problem, I often start by evaluating similar (and dissimilar) pieces I've built in the past.

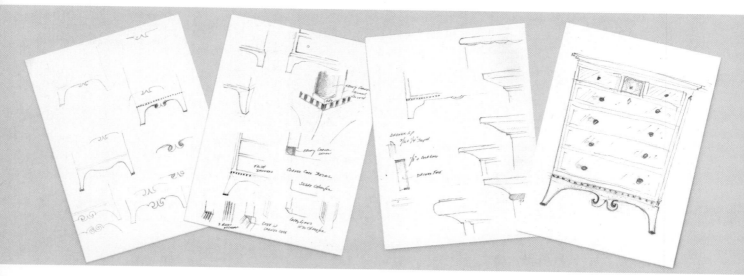

DETAILS, SUCH AS INLAID handling,
embellishing the apron, and contrasting woods, add original touches
to a basic chest of drawers.

The most exciting designs are those with the fewest restrictions. For example, a man recently gave me a commission for a chest of drawers. He didn't have any fixed ideas of what he wanted. He favored cherry, but he was open to other light-colored native woods. He also liked the dimensions of another chest he owned, about 4 ft. high and a little less than 3 ft. wide.

Find a Starting Point

Designing a chest of drawers shouldn't be all that complicated, considering that it's basically a series of boxes that slide into a larger box. Thinking about wood choices is often a good place to begin the design process. Dark woods can make a large chest seem heavier, just as light woods have the opposite effect. Chests have a lot of surfaces—the sides, top and drawers—that show off a wood differently than, say, the linear parts of a chair. Lots of heavy grain can dominate and distract from the quieter details. Fine-grained hardwoods take and hold small details that time would deface in

a softer wood like white pine. With its quiet grain and rich color, cherry would have been a good choice for the client's chest of drawers, but I was a little tired of seeing it everywhere.

Butternut, another native species, soon came to mind. Commonly called white walnut, butternut has a warm amber color, subtle grain, and works nicely with hand tools, although it's a little soft. I also had three exceptional wide boards stashed away—just enough to make single-board case sides and the top.

The widest case sides I could get out of the butternut boards were about 20 in., and the width of the top was limited to about 22 in. That size would allow drawers of a good usable depth. Defects in the boards limited the sides to 47 in. long. This would allow for a stack of five ample drawers. Four feet is also a nice height to stand at to see and use the top of the chest. Remembering that my client liked a chest of similar height, I used it as a starting point, drawing front and side views to proportion the drawers.

Developing the Design

The smallest practical clothes drawer is about 4½ in. deep. Drawers deeper than 9 in. to 10 in. are prone to being overloaded and are not that efficient (imagine trying to find a particular shirt in a drawer with shirts stacked five high). I don't use any magic proportioning system for drawers; I just sketch out ideas. Sometimes it's as simple as increasing each successive drawer by an inch. Arranging larger drawers at the bottom and smaller drawers at the top is not only practical but also balances the composition. To give interest to the facade of this chest, I tried breaking up the top tier of drawers. First I tried two and then three smaller drawers. This seemed more flexible in terms of storage and created a small drawer perfect for small treasures. Should the facade of drawers be flush, lipped, flat or

Finding the Right Proportions

The visual balance of the parts can sometimes be so subtle—they just feel right. Awkward proportions are often more obvious. There are a few guides to help you find pleasing proportions, but it is best to train your eye by looking critically at good design of all kinds.

35½ in.

20¼ in.

4¾ in.

5⅝ in.

6¾ in.

47⅞ in.

7⅝ in.

Case tapers from 33⅞ in. at base inlay to 32¾ in. at top.

8¾ in.

9⅛ in.

35⅜ in.

Case front bows 2 in.

shaped into a gentle bow front? As I developed other parts of the design, I would have a better idea about this.

The next problem was figuring out which base to use. I wanted a base that gave the massiveness of this chest a lift, maybe even to the point of exaggerating it a little. Too low a base would have given the chest a squat and heavy feel. Drawers close to the floor are also less comfortable to use. A high base cuts into the storage volume, but the visual lift it gives to the design more than makes up for this.

An idea that immediately appealed to me was four gently splayed feet known as French feet. Sometimes they splay to the side, and other times they splay forward as well. French feet create a sense of spring or tension, lifting the case. Flowing in an uninterrupted curve from the case, they would nicely complement the simplicity of the single-board sides. Quite foolishly (because I did not think about how much extra work this would be), I had the idea of emphasizing that upward curving energy by tapering the chest slightly, narrowing it at

the shape of the case, drawers, and base, the most likely differences would be in the details.

While the larger elements of form and proportion might catch your attention, the details keep you interested. Edge shapes, moldings, inlays, touches of color, and even the feel of surfaces can encourage your eyes and hands to play over a piece of furniture and come to know it more intimately. The details can often be a starting place for a design, or in this chest, a way to draw the various elements together. The challenge is to provide plenty of details to explore while maintaining a harmony among those de-tails. Similar to a musical fugue, they should be variations of a theme.

The base illustrates the movement de-tails can create. The drawback to the French feet was that your eye could follow the curve of the side and foot right to the floor and dead end there. Little ebony pads on the bottom of each foot catch your atten-tion before this happens. The vibrant black and the tiny bead cut along the bottom edge of the toes relate them to the cock-beads around each drawer and the ebony corner columns. Moving your gaze back up, the inlay band at the bottom of the case draws your eye horizontally around the two sides and facade. To draw more attention to the base and to relate this chest to earlier chests built in the area where my client lived, I carved the whale's tail details. They express some of the same curving energy as the feet and bow fronts, and perhaps propel your eye upward.

the top. In the drawings, I played with an inch or more taper, just on the edge of perception.

Why French feet rather than a more tra-ditional design of a molded bottom edge of the case with bracket feet? Adding on the base in this way would have solved some of my problems with the defects at the ends of the case side boards and allowed me to build a higher chest. But such a base inter-rupts the smooth, upward sweep of the case, something my evolving design was emphasizing. I was also beginning to think about bowing out the drawers slightly, a curve echoing the out-swept feet.

Get Down to Specifics

At this point I had the beginnings of a de-sign: a primary wood, rough dimensions of the case and drawers, curving French feet, and possibly bow-front drawers. I had a good idea of how I might build the chest using single-board parts. Nothing was cast in stone. I could only imagine how differ-ently a Shaker brother or an 18th-century Boston cabinetmaker would have worked within similar parameters and the vastly dif-ferent chests they might have created. While there may be obvious differences, such as

Practical Reasons Behind Details

The details that keep you exploring the forms can evolve for very practical reasons. Cockbeads, proud beads around drawer edges, originated as a way to protect the fragile veneered facade of the drawer. Using them meant flush, not lipped, drawers. Because I had only one other board from the same tree as the sides and top and I wanted good color and grain match, a solution was to laminate the drawer faces. I could then use any butternut for the backing laminates. Adding a cockbead allowed me to hide the lamination lines and nicely define the edges of each drawer. The cockbead also helps hide the necessary gap around the drawer in its opening and some of the slight variation of how the bow-front drawer aligns with the facade. Laminating the drawer faces into a bow front was only slightly more work and makes for a more interesting design.

By the time I had envisioned a pattern of ebony contrasted with holly and butternut, the rest of the details followed. Ebony corner columns give those edges definition and the case more verticality. The small ebony center drawer with a holly knob attracts your eye to the center of the facade and to the curved top. The top's modest overhang draws a minimum of attention; under-beveling the edge presents a thin and elegant profile. The coved under-bevel repeats the similar curves of the legs and bow fronts. The small cove molding under the top smooths the transition from top to case. Ebony knobs are practical and add interesting dots of color.

I like to add details so subtle that they will be discovered only by a casual sweep of your hand someday. The ebony backsplash has such details—it balances the ebony feet and echoes the overall color pattern with the noticeable holly dots at the ends. Almost hidden between the dots is a very fine groove and bead cut along the top edge. Whoever finds the bead might find the small tapering chamfer defining the back edge of the backsplash as well.

Every furniture design is an experiment of sorts. You have to define the problem and pursue solutions that give you hints at a

direction to keep going. Trusting your decisions is part of maturing as a designer. But what keeps it all interesting is the serendipity of furniture making. You can't foresee everything. I didn't plan the slight cant of the knobs down the front, but I like them.

GARRETT HACK is a frequent contributor to *Fine Woodworking* magazine.

TO BALANCE THE SPLAYED base, the top needs some overhang and mass, but not necessarily the mass of a thick top. The top is thick; but by covering its underside and adding another small cove molding, its profile is more elegant and interesting. The main cove is subtle and far enough below eye level that the author hopes it might be discovered as much by feel as it would by sight.

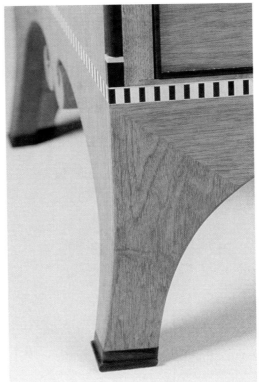

MORE EXCITING THAN CHAMFERING or rounding the corners of the case, quarter-round ebony and holly columns boldly define these edges. They also help emphasize the verticality of the case and lead your eye to the upwardly sweeping French feet. Rounded columns echo the beads around the drawers and the ebony pads on the feet.

Sideboard Strategies

BY WILL NEPTUNE

IT IS ALL TOO EASY to sketch something that looks good, only to discover that you have no reasonable way to build it. You either develop overly complex construction methods or sacrifice the design you really want because it's too difficult to build. The solution is to strike a balance between design complexity and construction simplicity. It helps to start by thinking of a piece in its most basic form, then develop a single construction system that can accommodate a wide range of design options.

I like to tell my students at North Bennet Street School that a sideboard is little more than a box with legs attached. Though it sounds oversimplified, this approach puts things in familiar terms—everyone knows how to build a box. It becomes a question of how to build the better box. Historically, sideboards were built using post-and-rail or frame-and-panel construction, but I prefer this method, which calls for a dovetailed box turned on its side. My alternative approach is less familiar, but when you start counting the joints necessary to build a frame-and-panel sideboard, you understand the logic of a dovetailed design. With this method, there are fewer joints to cut, and the ones you do cut aren't seen, so there's no need to be overly meticulous.

This construction system is based on a few rules concerning joinery: If a case part joins another at a corner, dovetail it; if one part meets along another's length, use multiple tenons. Dovetails and tenons are both strong joints that allow for wood movement and resist racking. Because all of the structural parts of the case have grain running in the same direction, the case expands and contracts together. Put simply, the case is still just a long, dovetailed box with legs attached.

Sideboards built using this approach may vary in size, line, and style, but they

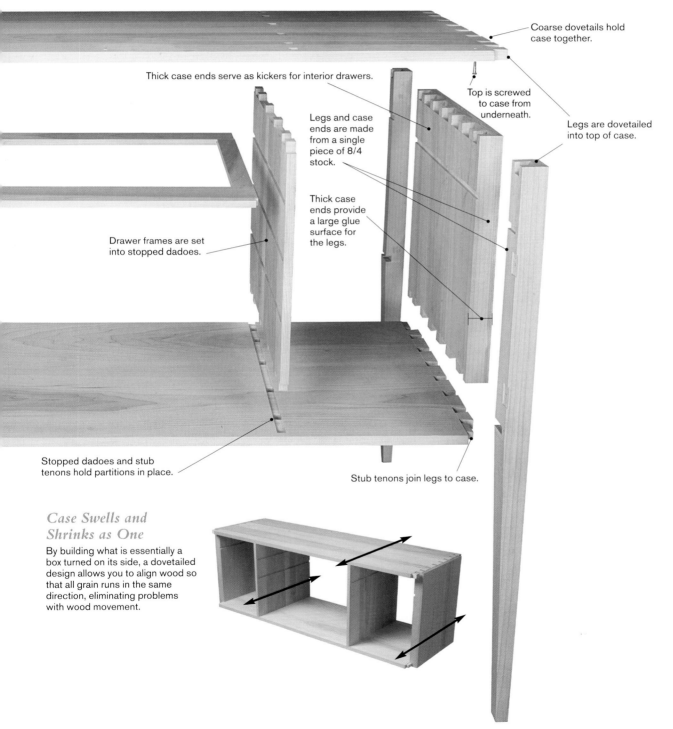

Coarse dovetails hold case together.

Thick case ends serve as kickers for interior drawers.

Legs and case ends are made from a single piece of 8/4 stock.

Top is screwed to case from underneath.

Legs are dovetailed into top of case.

Thick case ends provide a large glue surface for the legs.

Drawer frames are set into stopped dadoes.

Stopped dadoes and stub tenons hold partitions in place.

Stub tenons join legs to case.

Case Swells and Shrinks as One

By building what is essentially a box turned on its side, a dovetailed design allows you to align wood so that all grain runs in the same direction, eliminating problems with wood movement.

1. Built-Up Ends

Using the Grain to Make Invisible Joints

By carefully planning the cuts, a single 8/4 board can be laid out to form leg-and-end assemblies that appear to be a single, solid board. The legs are cut from the straight-grained edge of the board, and the ends are book-matched and laminated from resawn stock. When the legs join the ends, you're left with virtually invisible gluelines.

1 Proper left front leg
2 Proper right front leg
3 Proper left rear leg
4 Proper right rear leg
5 Left end blank
6 Right end blank
X Marks top ends of pieces

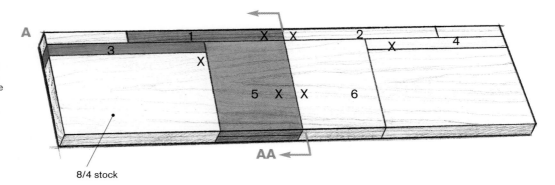

Legs and end-stock for both assemblies is laid out on a single board.

8/4 stock

Once the ends have been laminated, legs and ends are planed at the same time to ensure uniform thickness.

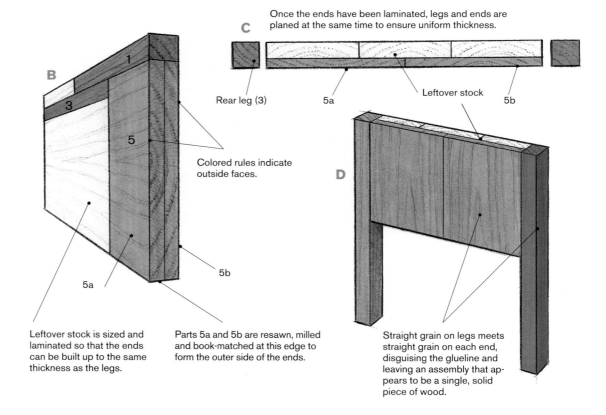

View of end grain at section AA

Colored rules indicate outside faces.

Rear leg (3)

5a

Leftover stock

5b

Leftover stock is sized and laminated so that the ends can be built up to the same thickness as the legs.

Parts 5a and 5b are resawn, milled and book-matched at this edge to form the outer side of the ends.

Straight grain on legs meets straight grain on each end, disguising the glueline and leaving an assembly that appears to be a single, solid piece of wood.

2. Dovetailed Box

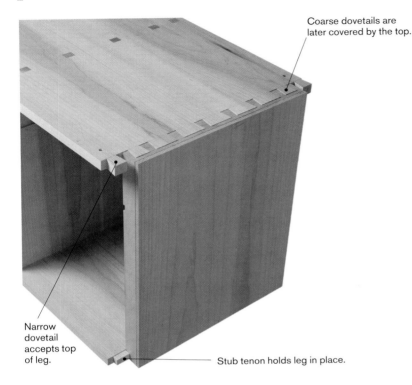

Coarse dovetails are later covered by the top.

Narrow dovetail accepts top of leg.

Stub tenon holds leg in place.

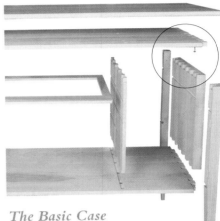

The Basic Case

A simple dovetailed box is modified to accommodate the legs. Dovetails can be cut coarse (with wide pins and tails) because the top will later cover them. Narrow tails at the front and back of the top and stub tenons at the case bottom are later fit to the legs.

retain a family resemblance based on the construction system. The mocked-up sideboard shown on these pages is the most basic variation of this system, but it lays a foundation that can be used on more complex designs. Once you understand the construction system, you can focus on design and build in styles ranging from Federal to Arts and Crafts.

Basic Sideboard Design

A sideboard is typically a tall case piece that's often 40 in. high and taller, a convenient working height for a standing person. The height of a sideboard makes anything displayed on its top more visible because it isn't overpowered by the forest of chairs surrounding a dining-room table. A sideboard is also strongly horizontal because the tall legs hold the mass of the case off the floor and because the case length exceeds the height. The open space below the case keeps the sideboard from appearing too massive, an effect you get with many large case

pieces. With lengths of 4 ft. and 5 ft. being common, the facade can be divided using a combination of drawers and doors (see the drawings on p. 116).

In designing the mocked-up poplar sideboard seen on these pages, I wanted a simple piece with a country feel. In form, it refers to the Federal period but avoids the use of veneers, inlay, and hardware seen in period, high-style examples. To simplify construction, I decided on a small, four-legged version without the curved facade often seen in Federal examples. Country furniture makers made similar design choices in earlier times, using the grain and figure of local woods or even painted finishes to give a piece visual interest. These designs rely on proportion and line to create a sense of balance and harmony.

The Construction System

One key feature of this construction system is the use of built-up ends, which are thick-

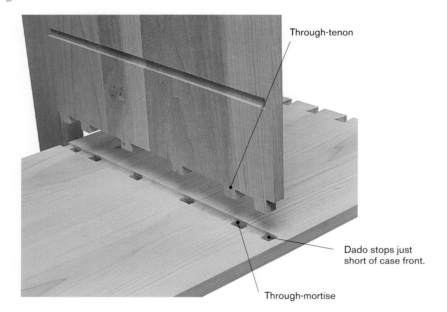

Through-tenon

Dado stops just
short of case front.

Through-mortise

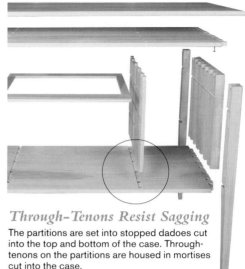

Through-Tenons Resist Sagging
The partitions are set into stopped dadoes cut
into the top and bottom of the case. Through-
tenons on the partitions are housed in mortises
cut into the case.

nessed to the same dimension as the legs.
The thicknesses of the ends provide large
glue surfaces for the legs. In addition, the
top and bottom join the legs and ends
without having to be notched around the
legs. This structural solution creates a lined
interior for the cupboard areas.

The partitions that divide the facade are
not only design variables, but they are also
structural elements. The multiple stub
tenons tying the long top and bottom together eliminate sagging almost completely.
All of the drawers run on frames let into
stopped dadoes.

In a real project, if saving primary wood
is important, all of the case parts other than
the legs can be made of a secondary species
and faced or edged with your primary
wood. Using a less dense secondary species
also saves weight.

Using built-up ends

Even though this entire mock-up is made
of poplar, I laminated the ends the same
way I might for a sideboard built in cherry
or mahogany. By resawing a piece of

8/4 stock, you're able to show a book-
matched pattern on the ends. The inner part
of each end is glued up from the leftover
pieces of the 8/4 stock. This is a nice way to
keep the legs from appearing as though they
were stuck on as an afterthought. This effect
is enhanced by good grain matches on the
legs and ends, which make each assembly
look like one solid piece (see the drawings
on p. 112). This is particularly effective if
you can choose an 8/4 board that is flatsawn and wide enough for the edges to
have growth rings running at about 45° (as
seen on the end grain). This gives you
straight grain on the legs, which helps disguise the glueline. As a bonus, the adjacent
faces of the legs also match each other.

In the mock-up, I resawed the 8/4 stock
thin, trying to avoid the green heartwood,
but the thickness of the layers doesn't matter. The object is to calculate the width of
each end so that little wood is lost between
the ends and the legs, which would disturb
the grain match. Also, you must start thick
with both layers to allow for later milling.
Once the inner and outer layers have been

4. Dovetailed Legs

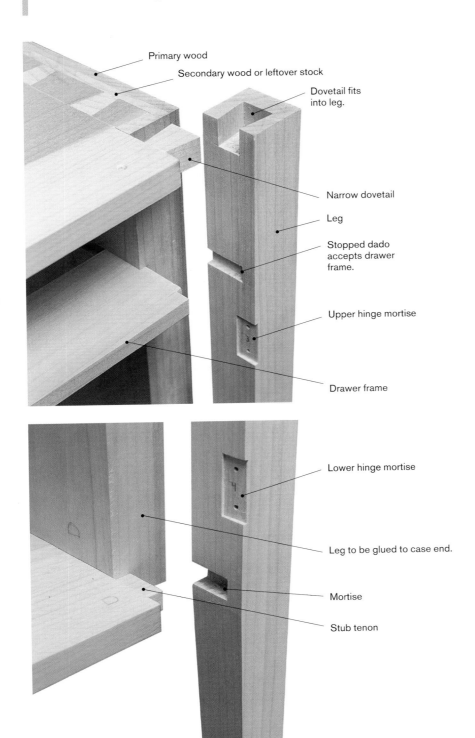

Primary wood

Secondary wood or leftover stock

Dovetail fits into leg.

Narrow dovetail

Leg

Stopped dado accepts drawer frame.

Upper hinge mortise

Drawer frame

Lower hinge mortise

Leg to be glued to case end.

Mortise

Stub tenon

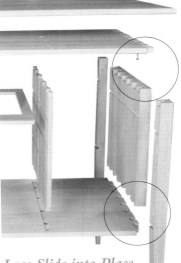

Legs Slide into Place

By housing each leg in a narrow dovetail at the top of the case and a stub tenon at the bottom, the leg can be slipped into place from underneath after the basic case has been assembled. Stopped dadoes are cut to accept the drawer frames. Cutting the dadoes with ends and legs clamped up before assembly ensures perfect alignment. The exposed top is screwed to the top of the case from underneath.

Finding the Right Proportions

With a sideboard, as the case gets larger and the negative space between the legs grows smaller, the piece begins to look more massive. But take a look and compare cases 1 and 2. Case 1 is far more delicate in size, but the case divisions give a static effect because they are based on squares and 2:1 rectangles. Although case 2 is much bigger, both the vertical rectangles of the doors and the graduated drawer sizes help relieve any sense of heaviness. What if the drawers were the same size and the doors more square?

Putting the doors on the outer parts of case 3 leaves the drawer compartment overpowered, at least to my eye. Even though the initial placement of the partition gives equal divisions, once the central space is divided, it looks too small.

Case 4 uses proportions that I often rely on. Leaving 50% in the middle gives a strong impression but is not as obvious to the eye as halves or thirds. Dividing the total sideboard height in half is also satisfying but remarkably subtle because it takes a moment to see the relationship of the positive space to the negative. Overall, I like the interplay of vertical and horizontal rectangular spaces. But I would still be willing to adjust things by eye to get a more pleasant drawer spacing, for instance. For me, it's less important that the height be exactly divided in half than it is for the divisions of space to produce an impression of these proportions.

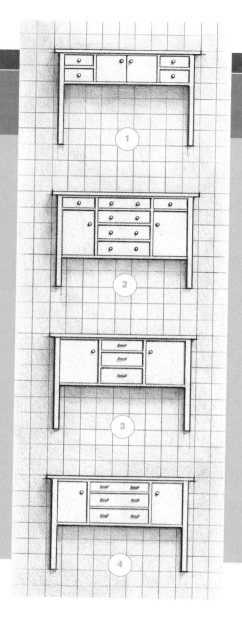

edge-glued, skim them with a handplane before gluing them together.

Alignment is much easier if you leave the parts long at this stage. The extra length allows you to nail the parts together in the waste areas when you clamp them up. The laminated parts should be given several days to move and reach equilibrium. After they are done moving, both the leg blanks and the ends can be flattened and thicknessed at the same time. When you trim the ends to finished length and width, remember to keep the book-match line centered and parallel to the edges.

Dovetailing the case

The top and bottom of the case are milled and glued up like any large panels, then cut to final size. The dovetails that hold the case together are fairly easy to cut, either by hand or machine, but remember that the layout is different at each corner where a leg joins the case (see the photos on p. 113). The top rear dovetails are cut narrow to make room for the back boards where the leg will be rabbeted. The case bottom has stub tenons that will be housed into the legs. These tenons are shouldered so that any later sanding won't change the fit of the joints. Once the piece is finished, none of the joinery will be visible, so the dovetails can be coarse (with wide pins and tails).

Filling out the facade

The partition joints are somewhat fussy to cut, but they add considerable strength to the case (see the photos on p. 114). Shallow stopped dadoes are used to locate the partitions. Tenons are positioned on the partition ends so that there is extra holding power at the edges with enough tenons across the middle to help the top and bottom resist sagging. The partitions are held in line by the dadoes, which makes fitting the thickness of the partitions to the dadoes careful work. Partitions should be cut a bit longer than the ends to leave some extra tenon length for final flushing.

Because the partitions are fully housed in the dadoes, there are only small shoulders at the front. It is very important that when clamped, the tenon shoulders bottom out in the dadoes, keeping both the top and bottom of the case parallel. Router planes can be fussy, but because the depth should be consistent, I took the time to run one through the dadoes of the mock-up.

To gauge the front shoulders, work in from both ends with a cutting gauge at the front until what's left between the lines equals the distance between the base of the pins cut on the case ends. Then add the depth of the dado and mark the space between the tenons. The trick is to get the small front shoulder to close at the same time that the end grain between the tenons bottoms out in the dado. This ensures that the top and bottom will remain parallel.

Once the tenons have been cut, locate the mortises in the dadoes. Line up the fronts of the partitions with the front of the case and mark around the tenons to establish your mortises. There is no need to run the tenons through, but it does add strength and keeps you from having to clean the bottoms of the mortises. When the partitions fit squarely into place, you've finished framing the basic case.

Attaching the legs to the case

The legs are mortised to accept the stub tenons cut into the bottom board (see the photos on p. 115). Because these tenons and the top dovetails share the same shoulder line, the legs should register flush to the case ends. Once the top dovetails are let into the legs, you can't trim any more wood off the legs and ends, so make sure this joint is accurate before you cut it. This method puts one serious requirement on the legs. They can be sawn to shape, turned or carved, but the solid glue surfaces must meet the case ends.

To guarantee alignment, it's best to cut the dadoes for the drawer dividers using a router with the case ends and legs clamped up. Once the stopped dadoes have been cut, the case construction becomes fairly ordinary. Mortise-and-tenon frames that separate the drawers are glued in the front 3 in. or so but not at the back. Leaving space at the back ensures that when the case shrinks the frames don't push against the back of the case. Both the frame-and-panel doors and the dovetailed drawers are built using the usual methods, but I put small vertical stops behind the doors.

Construction Basics Remain Unchanged

No matter how you change the design, the rules of construction are simple—dovetail joinery is used at all corners, and multiple through-tenons are used where a board joins another along its length.

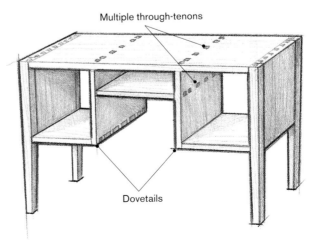

Multiple through-tenons

Dovetails

Decorative Apron Adds to Design

With the primary wood cut long and glued onto the secondary wood, an apron is formed and can be accented with scrollwork inlay. Cutting the secondary wood shorter allows you to employ the simple construction methods used on the basic case of the mock-up.

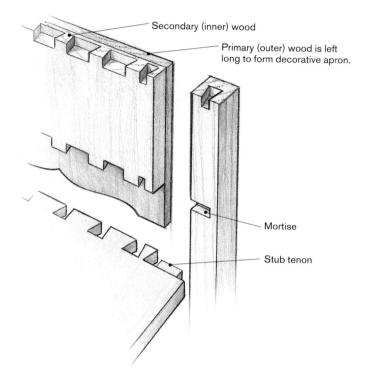

Secondary (inner) wood

Primary (outer) wood is left long to form decorative apron.

Mortise

Stub tenon

The rear legs and the bottom are rabbeted to accept the back. The back on the mock-up is a series of ¼-in. panels held by rabbeted cleats that are attached with screws. The top is ripped even with the bottom of the back rabbets so that the back boards run up to the exposed top. (This is not critical, but it does make it easier to fit the back.) A more elegant solution would be to resaw thin shiplap boards and run them vertically across the back. The top can be cut to allow some overhang, then molded and screwed down from below.

Alternative Constructions

There are a number of places where construction can be altered to save wood or to produce a slightly different effect. People are often surprised by the use of a full-board top and bottom. While it does use extra wood, it also adds strength to the case, resists cupping at the ends, and provides built-in kickers for the top drawers.

As a substitute, you could use two wide rails, with gussets or without. If your design has no cupboard space, you could use similar rails at the bottom. To allow for wood shrinkage, remember to fit any kickers with gaps at the shoulders and leave the rear tenons unglued.

The case ends could also be thinner than the legs, creating either a reveal where the ends join the legs or a recessed nook inside the case. Because of the added complexity of the case dovetails and drawer frames in the latter option, I would use it only if saving weight or wood is an issue.

It's easy to add decorative aprons between the legs (see the drawing at left). At the lamination stage of making the case ends, glue on the outer layer long at the bottom. This creates a large lap for the dovetails, which, as before, are cut flush on the inner layer of the end. The outer layer hangs down and can be sawn to shape. To add an apron across the front, the bottom can be cut back and an apron piece glued onto the edge of the bottom. If the apron is wide at the center, it can be braced from behind. If it is wide at the leg, it should be tenoned into the leg to prevent racking and twisting.

The most common change to the case is to have the bottom step up in the middle. This introduces movement, breaks up the strongly horizontal case, and allows different ways of arranging the doors and drawers. This type of case construction is more complex, but it uses the same joints as before (see the drawing on p. 117). Just remember how this system works: If a case part joins another at a corner, dovetail it; if a part meets along another's length, use multiple tenons. When you add a step up in the center of the case, only the fitting sequence changes.

First cut and fit the multiple stub-tenon joints between the inner verticals and center bottom panel. All of the stub tenons can be cut at the same time, but put off dadoing the top until the center panel is in place. The important thing here is to keep the inner verticals parallel. If the center panel clamps up shorter than planned, it's easier to move the dadoes in the top board (and make the center section smaller) than it is to live with verticals that aren't perpendicular to the case.

Now fit the dovetails of the ends to the top. While cutting the outer bottom panels, you can make any necessary adjustments. The most important thing is to keep the verticals parallel. Many things can creep in to change the exact locations of the verticals, but the top now tells you the actual distance between the inside faces of the verticals, a measurement that is more important than the overall length of the bottom pieces. So if the bottom location changed or you cut the bottom a bit short, adjust the gauge line for the dovetails until the distance between them is the amount required. The slight change of length in the tails is absorbed in the lap of the pin piece. As before, the space below the raised center section can be filled with decorative apron pieces.

Proportions and Style

In designing a sideboard, it's important to consider the visual effect that the proportions and construction methods will have, then choose ones that help express the intent of the design. Before considering any decorative effects, sketch a few cases of different sizes and proportions. Then use tracing paper to try out a variety of partition locations and to vary the door and drawer sizes. This exercise gives you a sense of how changes in proportion alter the effect. You may find yourself discarding all of these sketches, preferring to develop a second set using your eye to judge correctness.

Back Rides in Rabbeted Cleats

Rabbeted cleats are screwed to the rear top and bottom of the case. Three panels of ¼-in. plywood slide easily into place.

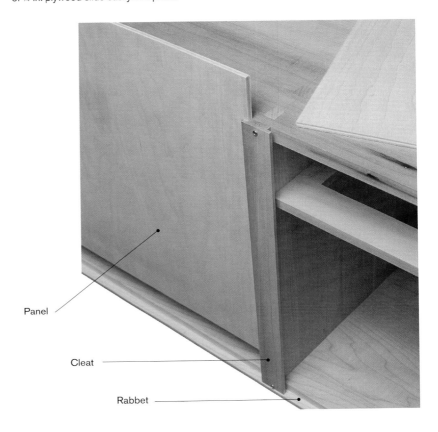

Panel

Cleat

Rabbet

The methods used on the mocked-up sideboard should provide the basics of construction. Most of the alternatives discussed don't really change the construction methods much. They are additions to the basic case that either save wood or provide surfaces for design options. More complex cases are possible, but they are all offshoots of this basic method. You can choose details to design a sideboard with a refined period look, or opt for something more contemporary.

WILL NEPTUNE teaches woodworking at North Bennet Street School in Boston, Mass.

Designing on the Go: A Coffee Table Takes Shape

BY PETER TURNER

MY SISTER WENDY offered me a deal I couldn't refuse. She'd give me one of her watercolor paintings if I made a worktable for her studio. She sent me a rough sketch showing a long, low table with a shelf beneath the top.

Then I started thinking. Why not turn Wendy's worktable into a prototype for something I could sell as a stock item in my booth at craft shows? Something everyone needs—a coffee table. This barter proved to be the start of a design-and-build process that produced four versions of this Shaker-style coffee table and culminated in the table you see in the front photo. It gracefully serves its purpose and is not difficult to build.

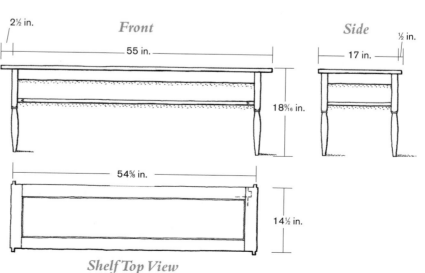

Shaker Simplicity in a Coffee Table

An ample overhang on the top, turned legs, and restrained design gives this coffee table a decidedly Shaker look. All joinery is mortise and tenon.

Front

2½ in.

55 in.

18⁹⁄₁₆ in.

Side

½ in.

17 in.

54⅝ in.

14½ in.

Shelf Top View

Small Changes Produce Big Results

Along the way, I tried three different leg designs, three approaches to the shelf and top construction, and several different dimensions on the top. Wendy's worktable, at 20 in. high, was a little too tall to correspond to most sofas. I lowered the second version to 18 in. and added a 48-in. by 23-in. top. The legs, turned from 1⅜-in. stock, were slightly tapered and ended at 1⁵⁄₁₆ in. at the floor (see the back table). Both the top and the shelf had breadboard ends. Although very useful, the table's narrow width reminded me of an aircraft carrier, and the legs ended up looking like cigars.

A shortened incarnation, 36 in. by 18 in., with square, tapered legs followed (see the center table). I added a more intri-cate breadboard design, one with multiple tenons, after I read an article by Garrett Hack describing his approach. That was as much to try a new technique as it was to provide more strength and stability.

But some of these design features made the table too expensive. So to make the table easier and faster to build (and as a result less expensive), I reduced its complexity while retaining its usefulness and grace. Breadboard ends were eliminated on the top and replaced on the shelf with a frame-and-panel design, which I think is easier to make. And along the way, I refined the turned leg from its initial cigar shape to a more delicate form. The first of these simpler versions was 18 in. high with a 48-in. by 18-in. top. I finally settled on a slightly longer version, with a 60-in. by 18-in. top that is ⁹⁄₁₆ in. thick. The shelf is ⅜ in. thick.

Simple Construction Complements the Design

There aren't many pieces to this table, and it doesn't require much material—in all, about 25 bd. ft. of 4/4 lumber and 4 bd. ft. of 8/4 wood for the legs. I use mortises and tenons to join both the apron pieces and the frame-and-panel shelf to the legs.

I start by turning the legs from 1¼-in.-sq. stock. I'm by no means a master turner, so I use only a few turning tools on the legs: a roughing-out gouge, a skew, a scraper, and a parting tool. The gouge does most of the work, and the only tricky part is turning the pommel at the transition where the leg goes from square to round. The danger is chipping out corners of the leg where it remains square. So I use the tip of the skew to make a shallow cut at the transition point (see the top photo on the facing page), then a scraper to round over the corners very gently. The detail I especially like is the ¼-in.-wide collar at the transition from round to square (see the inset photo on the facing page).

Once the legs are turned, I cut apron mortises in the legs and cut stile mortises in the shelf frame rails using a Multi-Router, which is a router-based joinery tool. But it doesn't matter how you cut the mortises. They could be done with a router, a mortiser, a drill press and chisel, or entirely by hand. I make grooves for the shelf in the frame parts on a tablesaw to match the mortises.

When I cut apron and shelf frame tenons, I make sure the length between shoulders on both apron ends and shelf rails is identical so the legs stay square. This means I make the long aprons first and then the shelf, which has a ⅜-in. by ⅜-in. tenon at each corner. I clamp a long apron between two legs and mark shelf mortises in the legs directly from the shelf tenons. Once the shoulder-to-shoulder distance on the shelf is established, I cut the short apron pieces to match.

When fitting the shelf panel, I take the shrinking characteristics of the wood and

KEEP TRYING. Peter Turner's work on this coffee table began with a request from his sister and a sketch (refer to opening photo). After several tries, he settled on a graceful design that he could build quickly.

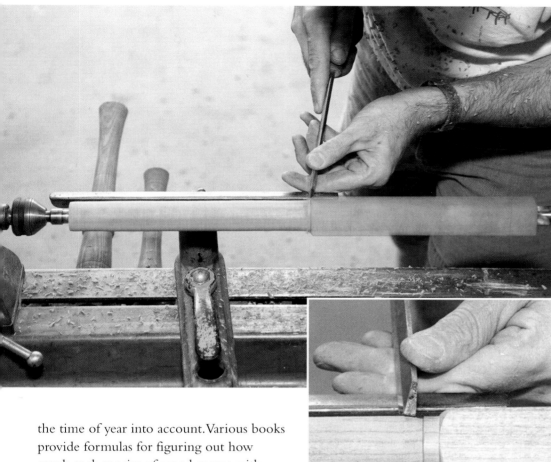

An early version of this turned leg was 13/16 in. dia. at the floor, but to the author, it looked too much like a cigar. He then developed this pattern, with a 1/2-in.-dia. foot.

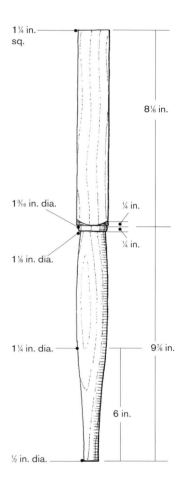

1 1/4 in. sq.

8 1/8 in.

1 3/16 in. dia.

1/4 in.

1/4 in.

1 1/8 in. dia.

1 1/4 in. dia.

9 7/8 in.

6 in.

1/2 in. dia.

the time of year into account. Various books provide formulas for figuring out how much each species of wood moves with changes in seasonal humidity.

I fitted the panel in this table in early October, when the weather was still warm, so I guessed the wood was close to its maximum width. The reveals around the edge of the panel are sized accordingly. The panel is flush on both sides of the shelf.

A tenon on each corner of the shelf fits into a corresponding mortise in the leg. I rough out these mortises on the drill press and clean them up with a chisel.

THE TOUGH PART IS THE TRANSITION. The point where the leg turns from square to round is easy to ruin. An initial cut with a skew can prevent chipping. A parting tool (inset) helps form the collar.

After Assembly, Finish Up with Citrus Oil

Final assembly begins with a dry-fit. Then I glue together the long aprons and legs. The short end aprons and the fully sanded shelf are then glued into place and pinned (I use 1/8-in.-dia. dowel for pins), two pins for each apron joint and one for each shelf joint. To attach the top, I use wooden buttons with tongues that fit biscuit slots cut on the inside edges of the aprons.

After bringing everything along to 320-grit sandpaper, I finish it with three coats of Livos oil, which has a pleasant smell and produces a nice satin sheen.

PETER TURNER makes furniture for a living in South Portland, Maine.

Making It Shaker
when the Shakers Didn't Make It

Can't imagine a living room without a coffee table? The Shakers could. They didn't build coffee tables. To give my design a feeling that is reminiscent of Shaker work, I turned to my reference library.

If you want to know more about the religious and social basis of Shaker craft, you can start with something called "Orders and Rules of the Church at Mount Lebanon: Millennial Laws of Gospel Statutes & Ordinances." This summary of Shaker habits—described in some of the books I used—was published for church elders in several versions between 1821 and 1887. Laws covered general approaches to furniture, and they could be very specific: The 1845 laws required beds to be painted green and limited bedroom mirrors to 18 in. by 12 in.

For the design of this table, I looked at photos of Shaker work. The greater the variety and number of photographic examples I absorbed, the stronger my vocabulary became in the elements of form, scale, proportion, and balance. This accumulated understanding allowed me to use specific design characteristics in this coffee table. Thin tops, ½ in. or ⅝ in., and ample overhangs, 2 in. to 3 in., on table ends are common on Shaker tables, so I adopted those elements here. The leg transition from square to collar to round came from a Shaker side table made in Enfield, N.H. Along with sound joinery and little decorative elaboration, the prudent selection of design elements evokes a harmony and balance present in the majority of Shaker work.

Joinery Is Simple and Effective

All joinery is mortise and tenon. Apron tenons, ⅜ in. thick and ⅞ in. long, are mitered at the corners.

2⅜ in.

Biscuit slot for buttons

The frame-and-panel shelf is completed before mortises for its ⅝-in.-sq. tenons are laid out on the legs. Shelf is ⅝ in. thick.

DON'T SKIP THE DRY-FIT. Gluing up all the table parts shouldn't be a nightmare. A dry run pinpoints problems while they can still be corrected.

Bun feet

Saber feet

Sled feet

Ogee bracket feet

Where Furniture Meets the Floor

BY MARIO RODRIGUEZ

DURING THE 1980s, when I operated a shop in Brooklyn, we received a steady stream of plain-Jane chests that had been picked up by interior decorators on their trips to the countryside or abroad. I was instructed to give these chests the "Cinderella treatment"—to revitalize them by changing the hardware, possibly adding stringing to the drawer fronts, or maybe making a new top.

By far the most dramatic change took place when I replaced a base. With a new base, a piece would assume a new personality. If I added just the right bracket feet, say, a mundane Victorian behemoth could be transformed into an elegant Chippendale-style treasure. The careful selection of the base proved, time and again, to be critical to the success of the completed piece. And I've found just the same thing to be true in designing my own pieces or adapting period designs.

To demonstrate the impact that different attached bases can have on a basic chest and to show how approachable most are to make, I've built a single, unadorned chest of drawers and fitted it with four different bases: with bun feet, with saber feet, with sled feet, and with ogee bracket feet. All four of these bases are drawn from historical examples, but as you'll see, they can easily be adapted to modern designs as well.

Bun Feet

A lathe-turned foot that has its origins in Europe, the bun foot is typically held to the bottom of a case by means of a wedged round tenon locked into a hole drilled into the case or into a molded frame below the case. A flattened section at the bottom of the spherical bun gives the foot a firm stance on the floor.

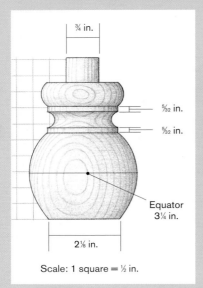

¾ in.

⁵⁄₃₂ in.

⁵⁄₃₂ in.

Equator
3¼ in.

2⅛ in.

Scale: 1 square = ½ in.

BUN FOOT STARTS WITH a gouge. Turn a rough cylinder, then use a pencil to mark out the major segments of the foot, including an equator for the foot's sphere.

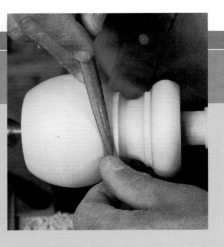

FINISH WITH A RASP. Use a rasp with a light touch to smooth the bumpy surface left by the gouge and to finish shaping the bun foot.

WRENCHING ACCURACY. To size the round tenon on top of the bun foot, hold an open-end wrench against the back of the foot while cutting the tenon to size with a parting tool. When the wrench slips over the tenon, it's the right size.

FOOTED FRAME. The round tenons of the bun feet are wedged to holes drilled in a molded frame. The frame is screwed to the bottom of the case.

Why You Need a Base

A chest is essentially a box on a base. The box is where the action is—the drawers, the doors, the shelving. So the base, resting right on the floor, might seem likely to fall beneath our notice. But its impact is strong. First, it literally lifts the cabinet off the floor. The air it puts beneath the piece gives the cabinet definition and makes even an armoire appear lighter. Plunked right on the floor without a base, a large cabinet looks stunted and incomplete; it begins to seem immovable, like a part of the building. A Newport secretary minus its bracket feet would be about as impressive as the Statue of Liberty standing knee-deep in New York harbor.

Saber Feet

The front feet on a Hepplewhite-style saber-footed base curve both to the front and the sides. The back feet curve only to the side, allowing the case to sit tight against a wall. Mortise-and-tenon joints hold together the rails and feet. Pine blocks strengthen corners. The base is screwed to the case through the blocks.

For the compound-curved front feet, trace the layout template on two adjacent faces (A and B) of a 2¾-in. square leg blank. The tracings should meet at the foot's bottom tip. For the single-curved back feet, you need to trace the template only on one side.

Scale: 1 square = ½ in.

2¾ in.

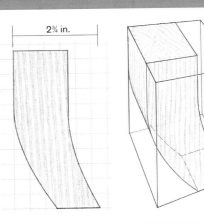

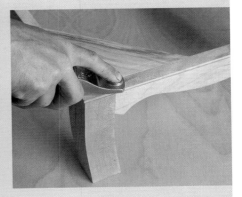

FRONT FEET ARE CUT four times. The front feet on a saber-footed base curve to the front and to the outside, requiring four bandsaw cuts. The first two cuts are made with the blank resting on the same face.

TAPE THE WASTE BACK ON. After making the first two cuts on the front feet, tape the waste pieces back on the feet. This will give you a flat surface on the bandsaw for the second two cuts.

BACK FOOT MEETS THE FRAME. Saber feet are often linked with rails to create a strong frame that's screwed to the bottom of the chest. The foot is trimmed flush to the frame with a block plane.

The proper base should not only elevate the case but also enhance the other features of it. Instead of concentrating all of the detailing on the case and treating the base as an afterthought, I work out the details of the base along with the case.

My choice of a base is influenced by the size and weight of the piece. For instance, I wouldn't place a massive, multidrawer chest on dainty saber feet. Structurally, the feet might not support the great weight of the piece and its contents. And aesthetically, a large cabinet supported by diminutive feet

Sled Feet

This base of European origin is made of three main components: two sled feet and a perpendicular beam. The front of the feet typically protrude beyond the front of the case. A ⅞-in. tenon is turned on each end of the beam, and it is secured through holes in the feet with a wedge (see the right photo below).

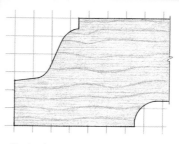
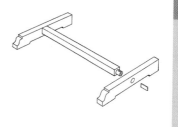

Scale: 1 square = ½ in.

CRISP CUTS START on a tablesaw. Cutting the shoulder on the front of the sled-footed base is best done on a tablesaw.

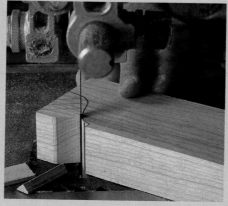

RELIEVING THE WASTE. Several bandsaw kerfs cut just to the layout lines of the front of the sled foot will make it easier to maneuver the wood around the blade for the tight corners of the finish cut.

WEDGE TREATMENT. The back of each sled foot is cut square and flush with the back of the chest. Both feet are screwed to the bottom of the chest.

might bring to mind a sumo wrestler wearing ballet slippers.

From a practical perspective, the lift a base provides also gives better access to the contents of a piece and protects them from moisture and dirt. In addition, an attached base can simplify construction of the carcase and can easily be replaced if it is damaged.

A Base with Bun Feet

The bun-footed base is a lively design that can animate even a very large piece of furniture. Yet with their low center of gravity and rounded form, bun feet are the sturdiest possible. The base is willing to carry great

weight and will even endure being shoved and dragged across the floor. The ball-shaped feet introduce a nice counterpoint to the rectilinear lines of a chest. The balls can be full and round, almost forming perfect spheres, flattened like doughnuts or elongated into cylindrical shapes.

Bun feet originated in Germany and Scandinavia and later were used on Kasten and blanket boxes in America. Bun feet were typically used on fairly massive pieces, but they found their way onto more refined case pieces such as desks and chests during the William and Mary period (1690–1730).

Bun feet are produced on the lathe. In the earliest examples, they were turned from a single block of wood; later, the block was laminated. Each foot has a stem or tenon at the top that is used for attachment to the case. Below that is a ringlike shoulder and then a narrow neck, called the reel, that swells into the ball. The most difficult aspect of turning a bun foot is executing a nice, round ball. If it looks like a potato, it won't work as a bun foot.

For a typical bun foot, start by turning a cylindrical blank. Mark out the major segments of the foot on the cylinder, including a line for the equator of the ball and a circle on the end of the cylinder to establish the flat portion where the ball will rest on the floor. Turn the reel and the shoulder first and then begin work on the ball.

Seasoned turners often use a large skew chisel to cut a sphere. By pivoting and rotating the tool, they obtain a smooth, arcing surface that requires little or no sanding. If you have less experience on the lathe, you might have better luck with a stout gouge. The surface you achieve may be a little bumpier, but the gouge is less likely to dig in and ruin the job because only a small portion of the tool's cutting edge contacts the workpiece. Even so, cut carefully, stopping frequently to check for symmetry.

You can use a rasp to perform the final shaping and smoothing. A rasp can be easily controlled and lightly applied to the rotating shape to correct the bun's outline. By varying the pressure, you can control the amount of wood you remove. And unlike a turning tool, the rasp won't dig into the work. Use sandpaper on the spinning piece to attain the final smooth surface.

There is a foolproof technique for turning the tenon on a bun foot to a precise diameter. From behind the rotating workpiece, press an open-end wrench against the tenon while removing material with a ⅛-in. parting tool. The narrow parting tool is used with a scraping action, so it doesn't require careful guidance and can be held in one hand. When the tenon is reduced to the precise final dimension, the wrench slips over the tenon.

The simplest way to attach bun feet to a case is to drill holes into the bottom of the carcase to receive the feet's tenons. But if the interior of the cabinet or chest will be visible, so will the ends of the tenons. In that case, attach the feet to a frame and then screw the frame to the underside of the chest. Make the frame of solid wood and cut a profile on its edge, which adds a molding to the bottom of the chest.

A Base with Saber Feet

The sleek, graceful saber foot was most popular during the Hepplewhite period (1790-1805), when Baltimore cabinetmakers used it extensively. But with its hard edges and simple sweep, the saber foot transcends period classification and looks perfectly comfortable on modern pieces. Visually, the saber foot works best with pieces that are moderate to small in size, fairly rectilinear in form, and restrained in detailing. On the right case, a base with saber feet will confer a sense of poised nimbleness, like that of a dancer.

When designing saber feet, strive for a smooth, moderate curve. Start by making a cardboard template of the silhouette and use the template to trace the silhouette on a square blank. For the front feet of the base, which curve to the front and to the side, trace the template on adjacent sides of the blank; for the back feet, which curve only to the side, trace the template only on one side of the blank. As you design the curve of the feet, err on the side of moderation; a curve that looks good on the template will often appear

Ogee Bracket Feet

Popular in the Chippendale period, ogee bracket feet are made from sections of tablesaw-made ogee molding. The tight inside curve of each foot is cut on a drill press before the rest of the bracket is cut on a bandsaw. The rear feet are molded on the sides only. Flat pine blocks butt to the end of the rear feet and allow the case to sit tight to a wall (see the drawings below).

SPLINE TIME. An ogee bracket foot is made of mitered sections of moldings and held together with splines. After cutting the corner miter on a tablesaw, the author sets up the saw to cut a groove for the spline, taking care that the height of the spline cut is lower than the height of the thinnest part of the ogee profile.

LOW, INSIDE CURVE. Most of the cutout work on the ogee bracket foot is done on a bandsaw. An exception is any tight, constant-radius curve, such as the one near the bottom of the foot, which is more easily cut with an appropriately sized Forstner bit.

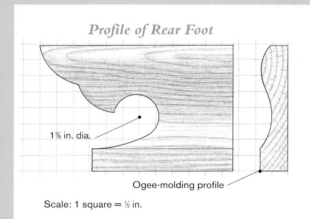

Profile of Rear Foot

1⅝ in. dia.

Ogee-molding profile

Scale: 1 square = ½ in.

TAPED AROUND A SQUARE BLOCK. To ensure a tight, 90° miter, set the splined-and-glued bracket foot around a squared block of wood. The miter is held tight with tape until the glue dries.

exaggerated when cut out of the blank, because each foot is a compound curve. Too radical a curve can make a foot look like it is straining under the weight of the cabinet. And, in fact, it may well be. The grain is short at the toe, and the farther the toe extends, the more vulnerable it is to breaking off.

The curves are cut on the bandsaw. After cutting one side of the front legs, temporarily reattach the cutoffs with masking tape. Then rotate the blank and cut the other curve. Clean up the convex curves using a block

plane with a very small throat opening and a very sharp blade. I do any further cleaning up with a card scraper. On the concave sides, I begin with a curved soled spokeshave and follow that with rasps and sandpaper.

Saber feet are often linked with rails, creating a strong frame that can easily be screwed to the bottom of the case. Like table aprons, the rails are tenoned on the ends and fitted into mortises in the saber feet. It is simplest to cut the mortises in the feet while the blanks are still square.

A Base with Sled Feet

Solid and low slung, the sled-footed base suggests—and delivers—stability and strength. It can be used on both low storage chests and towering cupboards. I've seen sled feet on painted Scandinavian chests dating back to the 15th century as well as on early 20th-century English Arts and Crafts pieces. To me, sled feet conjure up sturdy medieval coffers and cupboards reinforced with iron straps and hinges, or simple rustic furniture built and shaped with little fuss.

The sled-footed base is comprised of two parallel feet joined by a beam. The front ends of the feet typically extend beyond the front of the piece and are often chamfered, rounded over, or embellished with an ornamental scroll. A variation on this design that you sometimes see is one that raises the carcase off the feet with legs.

Because the shaped end of a sled foot is in front of the cabinet, its shape and finish must be crisp and attractive. Cut the shoulder of the scroll on the tablesaw and the curved outline on the bandsaw. Fair the curves and smooth them with fine rasps, files, card scrapers, and sandpaper. Start with a fine, 6-in. tapered rasp to create a flowing curve without any abrupt dips or blips. Work down from the bottom of the shoulder cut to the tip of the foot. Next, take care of the rough surface left by the rasp with a smooth round file and a card scraper. Finally, sand a bit for a silky surface. Make sure the curving edge is square to the sides, not lopsided. Refrain from breaking the edges, keeping everything crisp and clean.

Because the feet support the weight of the cabinet, the beam's purpose is mainly decorative. Not needing maximum strength, I joined the beam to the feet with round mortise-and-tenon joints. Turn the tenons on the lathe and size them with an open-end wrench to an exact ⅞-in. diameter. Then drill a corresponding hole in the feet to accept the through-tenon. For a decorative touch that also ensures a tight, clean joint, cut a thin kerf into the end of the tenon with a dovetail saw and later, when assembling the joint, tap a wedge into the kerf.

A Base with Ogee Bracket Feet

I always have fun with making ogee bracket feet and put great effort into their design. Ogee bracket feet give a rectilinear cabinet a fluid, sculptural touch, catching light and shadow in a pleasing way. This sculptural design was popular in the 18th century and typifies the Chippendale style (1760–1790). While displaying the sensuous nature of the wood, ogee bracket feet give a piece a sturdy, rocklike stance.

By definition, an ogee is a pair of complementary curves that form an S shape. The relationship of these curves can vary to suit your taste. The curves might be the same radius, or you might have a tight convex curve over a wide, shallow concave curve. The only requirement is that the convex curve be at the top and the concave curve below. A bracket foot with a convex curve at the bottom is called a reverse ogee.

A successful ogee profile will have a lively, curling contour, suggesting fabric unfurling. In addition to the undulating ogee, a bracket foot is defined by the profile at the end of each wing of the bracket. Some end quite simply; others end with a flourish of scrollwork. When designing a bracket foot, this end profile is read two ways—as a positive form (the foot) and as a negative form (the space beside the foot). You can explore this positive/negative relationship by cutting possible profiles in a light material and viewing them against a dark background.

SCREW THROUGH TRIANGULAR CORNER BLOCK. The back feet on an ogee bracket base are not mitered like the front ones. Rather, the ogee bracket butts a flat pine block that will be invisible when the case is placed against a wall.

Ogee Bracket Base Feet

Front Foot

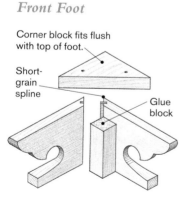

Corner block fits flush with top of foot.

Short-grain spline

Glue block

Rear Foot

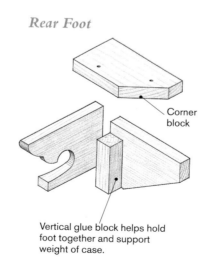

Corner block

Vertical glue block helps hold foot together and support weight of case.

There are a few ways to make ogee molding. I cut the cove with an angled fence on the tablesaw and the convex shape with tablesaw cuts and hand tools. After milling long sections of ogee profile, cut them into 8-in. lengths. Next, designate adjacent pieces to be paired up as feet so that the grain will be continuous around the mitered outside corner of the bracket. The pieces must be marked left and right to produce a pair.

I often use splines to register and align the joint. To cut a groove into the face of the miter, set the tablesaw blade to 45°. Clamp a scrap to the saw table to use as a stop to register the cut, and use the miter gauge to push the stock. Be careful to raise the angled blade no higher than the thinnest dimension of the ogee profile.

The grain orientation of the spline is critical to the strength of the joint: The grain should run across the width of the spline, not along the length. To produce a spline with the correct grain orientation, make a tablesaw kerf into the end grain of a scrap piece of molding. Then cut the spline free on the bandsaw. Most of the cutout work for the end profile of ogee bracket feet is done on the bandsaw. But to achieve a crisp result for designs that include tight inside curves, I begin at the drill press. I use whatever bit matches the radius I need—Forstner bits or circle cutters—to cut out the inside curves, then I cut the rest of the shape on the bandsaw.

MARIO RODRIGUEZ is a contributing edtior to *Fine Woodworking* magazine.

Dressing Up a Basic Box

BY ROGER HOLMES

MOST WOODWORKERS that I know spend three quarters of their time making boxes of one sort or another. Boxes for books, clothing, linen and blankets, dishes, cutlery, keepsakes, and odds and ends. We even spend a great deal of time making boxes for boxes, i.e., drawers for a chest or other case piece.

Designing with boxes is deceptively simple. First you figure out the right size and configuration of box or boxes to store or display the desired items. Then you try to make the boxes attractive. A recent request to build a pair of bedside cabinets for friends allowed me to explore methods of enhancing the basic box.

Wedged between the bed and a wall in many bedrooms, most bedside cabinets don't benefit from exposed joinery or lovely wood—you don't get much of a view of either. Trying to think outside the box, I started sketching various curvy alternatives, deciding on the simplest of them all—curving the front plane of the cabinet along a gentle arc. For centuries simple curves have been used to break the four-square rigidity of a box without sacrificing the advantages of rectilinear construction.

A good start, but it wasn't enough. I wanted to add some visual weight to the top and bottom, something a little more

MITERED CORNERS OF THIS cornice are not 45°. Take angle measurements for the curved front pieces from working drawings.

DOVETAILS ON THE SKEW. Holmes cuts the dovetails on the skew rather than flattening the face where the joint comes together. While tricky, it adds to the subtle details of superb craftsmanship of the piece.

PLINTH RAISES THE PIECE off the ground. The plinth makes the box look less like a box and provides a structural base for the cabinet.

substantial than the ⅞-in.-thick edges of the box. The solutions—a 5-in.-tall plinth and 2-in.-high cornice—are also traditional, even classical. As far back as the Egyptians, architects have used the plinth to raise a box off the ground and, in a sense, put it on display. They added a cornice on top, like a crown, terminating the structure with a flourish. Furniture makers have used both elements extensively.

My plinth is slightly larger than the box it supports, and simple moldings make the transition between the two elements.

A bead molding announces the beginning of the cornice. The body of the cornice is the same size as the box, but the grain runs horizontally on the sides, setting it off subtly from the vertical grain of the box below. Set in slightly from the cornice body, the cove-molded top panel finishes the job.

Construction Notes

Adding a curve, plinth or cornice is a time-consuming but rewarding way to make something special out of a simple box. I laminated the curved drawer front and rails for the plinth and cornice out of maple. I resawed the stock to about ³⁄₃₂ in. thick, then pressed the pieces between male and female forms made of medium-density fiberboard (MDF).

The plinth rails and legs were joined with mortise and tenons. Joining the curved front rail and leg required some careful layout but wasn't difficult to cut by hand or machine. The molding required slightly different cutter profiles for the curved and straight pieces to ensure an accurate fit at the corners. The molding was glued to the top of the rail-to-leg assembly. The plinth was screwed to the carcase through slots in the molding. The slots allow for seasonal movement.

The cornice was the trickiest element. I assembled the cornice frame, mitering the front corners. I attached the rabbeted cornice top to the frame, gluing the front edge and buttoning along the sides to allow for movement. Next, I attached the mitered bead molding to the carcase, gluing it down to the front edge and screwing it to the sides through slots, which allow the carcase to move. Finally, I glued the cornice assembly to the bead molding.

ROGER HOLMES is a former associate editor of *Fine Woodworking* magazine. He lives in Lincoln, Neb., where he publishes books and works wood.

An Elegant Case from Top to Bottom

Construction of this box is straightforward, except for the curved front. Holmes uses slotted holes for the screws where wood movement is likely to be an issue. The piece shown here is 18 in. deep by 19 in. wide by 28½ in. tall.

Cornice Detail

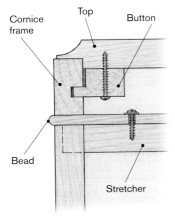

Cornice frame

Top

Button

Bead

Stretcher

Plinth Detail

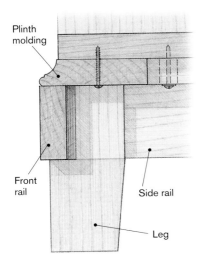

Plinth molding

Front rail

Side rail

Leg

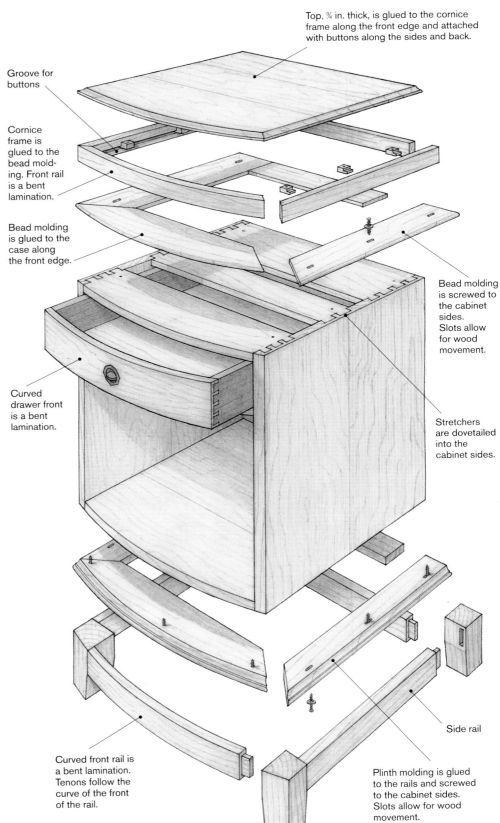

Top, ¾ in. thick, is glued to the cornice frame along the front edge and attached with buttons along the sides and back.

Groove for buttons

Cornice frame is glued to the bead molding. Front rail is a bent lamination.

Bead molding is glued to the case along the front edge.

Curved drawer front is a bent lamination.

Bead molding is screwed to the cabinet sides. Slots allow for wood movement.

Stretchers are dovetailed into the cabinet sides.

Side rail

Curved front rail is a bent lamination. Tenons follow the curve of the front of the rail.

Plinth molding is glued to the rails and screwed to the cabinet sides. Slots allow for wood movement.

Going Over Edges

BY WILL NEPTUNE

TOP EDGES ARE an opportunity, a chance for a furniture maker to reinforce and enhance the overall design of a piece: to emphasize the horizontal or vertical aspect, to draw attention away from the base and toward the top or vice versa, to repeat an element or quality of the base, or to take the piece in a new direction. But a top edge, whether on a table, a desk or a case piece, is not experienced in isolation. Rather, the edge affects you in concert with the rest of the piece.

An edge is a kind of hot spot, a place where the top and the base come together. An edge is also just one part of the top. When you design an edge, you must consider the size and the shape of the top, as well as the edge profile itself.

I'm going to look at 18th-century edges because they're the ones I'm most familiar with and because the 18th-century furniture makers worked out most of the moldings and edge profiles we're still working with today. If edges themselves are

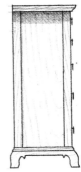

EDGE IGNORES BASE. **The shaped top of this Connecticut lowboy is a bold design (imagine the lowboy with a rectangular top), but there is little relationship between the top and the base.**

an opportunity, so too is the study of edges. Whether you build 18th-century reproductions or your own contemporary creations, a close look at edge treatments offers you a chance to add another set of options to your designer's tool kit.

The game of edge design is one in which little moves often have big consequences. Imagine two Queen Anne lowboys, similar in size and overall design. Both have rectangular tops with simple ogee moldings, but one has dimpled corners (see the drawing on the facing page). In the latter, the small, curved creases in the molding soften the edge and lessen the severity of the otherwise rectilinear top. Or imagine

that the top of a table you've made looks too thin once the edge has been molded. Should the top have been thicker or would a different molding have looked better? Either way, the slightest of alterations might have made all the difference.

Sizing the Top

When designing a tabletop, you should consider the size of the top before the shape of the top or the treatment of its edge. This is because you first take in the overall stance of a piece. You register the thickness of the top and the degree of its overhang long before you take in small-scale details such as the profile of the edge. From a distance, the elevation (front) view dominates the plan (top) view. A thin top tends to make the entire piece seem more delicate; a thick top tends to have the opposite effect. Large overhangs emphasize the horizontal; small overhangs allow you to grasp the relationship between the top and the base.

EDGE AMPLIFIES TOP. **In this pie-crust table, the top is intricately shaped in both plan view and in elevation. The concentric curves of the concave and convex edge carvings produce a pattern of inside and outside corners, enhancing the effect of the top's shape.**

EDGE EMPHASIZES ELEVATION.
The molded top edge and submolding on this Newport knee-hole desk read as one wide molding. The vertical quality of the wide molding emphasizes front elevation over plan view, directing the eye to the shells, which terminate the blocked design.

But the interaction of overhang and base is rarely so simple. As you come closer, a large overhang will block the view of the base. This limits opportunities for small edge details to tie the base and top together. So large overhangs tend to put a premium on plan-view design ideas. It may be enough for a large rectangular top to be made of beautiful wood: a single wide board or well-matched, figured wood. On such a table, a simple edge treatment will hold the viewer's gaze to the center of the top, emphasizing the wood itself.

Now consider a table or case piece for which you want to emphasize one elevation over the others, say a chest of drawers that will be viewed mostly from the front. The side overhang can be large, creating a strong horizontal effect from the front, and the front overhang can be small. The benefit of the small front overhang is that, as you come closer, your view of the base isn't cut off. Lowboys (see the left photo on p. 137) and block-front bureaus (see the bottom photo on the facing page) are both good examples

of this design idea. Even up close, the scrolled apron of the lowboy shows as well as the top. With the bureau, the focus on the stack of shaped drawers is reinforced by having a shallow front overhang shaped to match the curving pattern of the drawers.

If the overhang is kept small on all sides, a curious thing happens. The horizontal quality of the top is suppressed, and the overall visual effect is one of compactness, which can be seen in the Newport block-front desk (see the photo at left). A small overhang on the desk contributes to a compact stance and places the emphasis on the elevation.

Shaping the Top

In addition to the size of a top, the shape of a top in plan view provides another level of information to read along with the edge treatment. A top with a visually active shape leads the eye around its edge. If the edge itself has an interesting profile, the shape of the top can intensify the effect of the profile. Tripod pie-crust tables (see the right photo on p. 137) are a perfect example of this phenomenon.

Historically, shaping the tops of tables and case pieces was an expensive and desirable alternative to the more common rectangular top: embellishment equaled sophistication. However, I believe shaped tops proliferated due, as much as anything, to their dramatic visual effect. In many instances, a simple four-legged rectangular base would receive a shaped top to dress it up. Another approach was to have the base and top share a common form. The top becomes an extension of the base: The shaped edge functions as one more layer of concentric information.

By itself, a shaped top shows only in plan view; it essentially disappears in true elevation. But when moldings are introduced to the edge, a new effect develops. Patterns of shaped miters occur at every break from flat to flat, curve to curve or curve to flat. Often a shaped top develops a rhythm of inside and outside corners. This rhythm has a powerful visual effect on the edge. The more complex the molding, the more complex the intersections, and the more powerful the effect. If either the top or the molding was square, the effect would be lost.

Molding the Edge

Once you've looked at the way the size and shape of the top interact with both the top edge and the overall piece, you are ready to consider the edge itself. The design of an edge profile is all about curves or the lack of them. When it comes to designing curves (whether they're an aspect of an edge or of some other furniture element), there are those who prefer freehand curves and those who prefer compass-based constructions.

I certainly work with freehand curves, but I find myself reaching for a compass more often than not. I typically begin with either a tracing of an edge profile from a period piece or a rough freehand sketch of an edge profile I like. Then by careful observation and some guesswork, I try to find compass settings that will pass a line along the original. Many times two or three compass points will get me very close.

A curve that is pleasing to the eye is said to be fair. I've found that experimenting with a compass gives me a good sense of the character of fair curves. You can't kid yourself with a compass: either the radius lines of the two arcs share a common line or they don't. Flats or dead spots on a curve show up quickly with a compass because you can't get the curves to meet.

As a practical matter, designing edge profiles by using sections of circles enables you to use common, in-stock cutters to mold the edge. For short runs, I often find it quicker to cut an ogee with two router bits rather than to grind a large cutter. Using part of the curve of a core-box bit and shortening the wings of a quarter-round bit will allow you to mold ogees with little cleanup.

Over the years, I've observed a few fundamental principles for designing edge profiles: Round surfaces are softer-looking than flat surfaces; vertical lines and horizontal lines have a more severe effect than angled lines; 90° corners have a harder look than obtuse corners; the viewer of an edge reacts to shadow and light as much as to volume and shape.

In the glossary on pp. 140-141, I look at six basic edge profiles. The trick for the designer is to manage all the variables of the edge treatment while keeping an eye on the rest of the piece as well. A hands-on approach is the only way, ultimately, to discover the edge treatments that make sense for your work.

WILL NEPTUNE is a furniture maker and a woodworking instructor at the North Bennet Street School in Boston, Mass.

EDGE REPEATS BASE. The carefully matched veneer pattern on this Biedermeier tripod table leads the eye around the edge, making a direct visual connection between top and apron.

EDGE REINFORCES BASE. The blocking in this Boston block-front bureau is worked out through the entire elevation. The top edge is molded following a pattern of curves concentric to the drawer-front plan. The blocking design is reinforced by the top-to-base relationship.

A Glossary of Edge Profiles

SQUARE

This most basic edge shape is bold and simple. The single vertical surface will light up as a uniform plane or be uniformly in shadow.

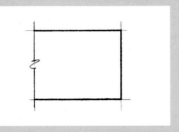

HALF-ROUND

The curve of the half-round (or bullnose) flows smoothly into the flat surfaces, softening the appearance of the edge. There are no hard surfaces or corners to interrupt the flow, but the price is the lack of clear boundaries.

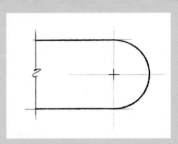

Though still a simple shape, the half-round seems more complex than the square edge because as you move around it, bars of light travel across its curved surface.

ASTRAGAL

The astragal begins as a soft half-round, but adds fillets to both sides. The combination of flats and a curve creates a bolder and more severe border than that of the segmental (at right). The added complexity of the flats makes the top appear thinner.

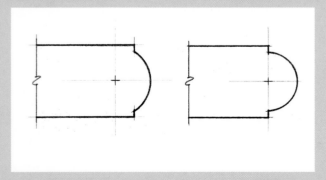

SEGMENTAL

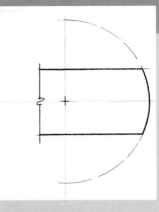

The segmental produces the same softness and sense of movement in light as the half-round, but the corners formed where the curve breaks at the flat win back some hardness and provide a definite border. Moving the compass point inward makes the edge a smaller piece of a larger circle; if the circle gets too large, the segmental appears as a square edge. But if the circle gets too small, the edge becomes, in effect, a half-round because the corners are less distinct.

THUMBNAIL

In a thumbnail edge, the curved surface is tipped, blurring the distinction between vertical and horizontal, yet the small top fillet provides a crisp border.

Moving the compass point down and to the left, as in the bottom thumbnail, generates a larger curve, flattening the edge profile.

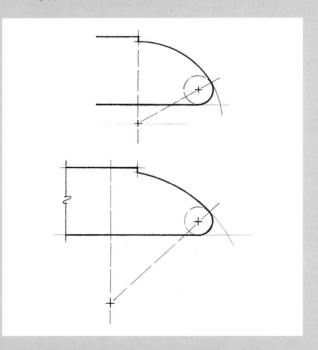

OGEE

The reverse curve of the ogee breaks the thickness of a top into several horizontal bands. This layered effect makes the top look thinner and more delicate. The concave and convex parts of the curve are perceived as separate elements, but because the transition is fair, there is no hard line to interfere with the feeling of softness. And yet, the crisp top corner provides a distinct border.

Ogees 1 to 3 have similar curves but different proportions. Increasing the radius of the upper, concave curve changes the overall proportions of the profile, making the half-circle nose appear pointier.

In ogees 4 to 6, the compass point for the concave curve moves upward. As the compass point moves up, the arc becomes less than a quarter-circle, and the top corner becomes more obtuse, making it softer and less defined.

A more subtle effect occurs where the concave and convex curves meet. If the convex curve completes a half-round, as in ogees 1 to 4, you sense the horizontal tangent line at the top of the curve. This comes across as a shelf, and gives the edge a harder, even harsh, look. Moving the compass point both upward and to the right, as in ogees 5 and 6, allows you to begin the upper, concave curve before completing the half-circle of the nose curve. This tips the tangent line away from horizontal and gives the resulting S-curve a more gentle feel.

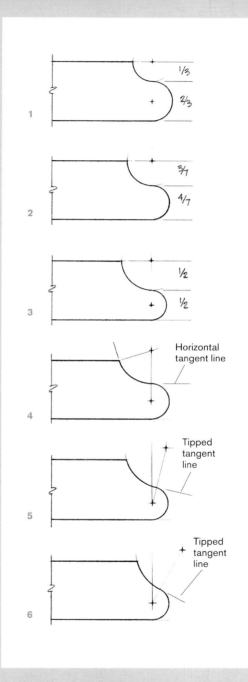

Designing Table Legs

BY GRAHAM BLACKBURN

MORE OFTEN THAN NOT, legs are the defining features of a table. Once you decide on the shape and color of a tabletop, making it is largely a question of providing the required surface area with the chosen stock. But the support for the tabletop is a different matter. Table legs—whether in the form of monolithic blocks, single pedestals, trestles, or in groups of three, four, or more—may be provided in a bewildering array of forms. The variety of legs is virtually endless, both from stylistic and construction standpoints.

Providing reliable support may be the most fundamental requirement demanded of any leg, but deciding on an appropriate form

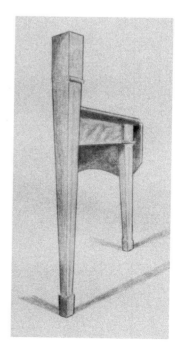

APPROPRIATE MATERIAL Some styles just beg for a particular wood species. For example, simple, square oak legs look great on a Mission-style table.

LIGHTNESS For a Shaker side table with a large overhang on the top and a narrow skirt, plain pine legs, tapered on two sides, lend a delicate look.

SOLID GROUNDING A weight-bearing library table built in dark walnut needs hefty legs, a solid skirt and bottom stretchers to support heavy loads of books.

SOBRIETY A Federal writing table built with deep walnut and mahogany tones calls for a restrained, classical leg design with stringing and a shaded holly inlay.

Stylistic Appropriateness

Right is a Federal-style leg (perfectly fine in its own right) that's unhappily married to a Mission-style table. The square leg at left is a more fitting choice.

Good

Oak

Mahogany

Bad

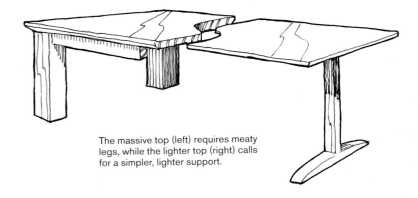

The massive top (left) requires meaty legs, while the lighter top (right) calls for a simpler, lighter support.

FLIGHTS OF FANCY Polychrome geometric solids add visual interest and a sense of humor to this large dining table of post-Memphis design.

and shape requires a reasoned understanding of the table's function and style. Whether you are designing with a certain period look in mind or venturing out into original designs, there is something to be learned by studying the furniture of the past. Frequently, period styles are characterized by features that produce distinguishing effects. If the purpose of these effects is understood, they can be duplicated in original designs that don't represent any particular period.

When planning a leg design, consider a few basic concepts that guide the process. Is the wood choice appropriate for the table design? Do you want the table to appear solidly grounded or delicate and refined? Should the table appear formal or relaxed? This article presents an overview of leg types, as well as their functions and construction methods, to make choosing a style and design easier for every table builder.

Function and Form

Very often a table's use will determine much of its leg design. The legs on a dining table, for example, must make sitting at it convenient: No matter how handsome any given leg may be, if it prevents a comfortable seating arrangement, it will be a functional failure. Similarly, if it is to be a heavy-load-bearing library table, it should not have

delicate, spindly legs. A table that must be movable, adjustable, or expandable should not rest on massive, stretcher-bound legs.

After a table's function has been taken into account, the question of style remains. Sometimes this merely means designing legs that are coherent with the table's essential character—stout, sturdy legs for a chunky, heavy-duty piece or delicate legs for a refined piece—but more often than not the table will contain references to a particular period or style. Adding inappropriately designed legs can result in an awkward combination that will spoil an otherwise soundly constructed piece.

Words like "inappropriately" and "awkward" may sound dangerously subjective, but in fact, style can be analyzed and understood quite objectively.

Design guidelines

When attempting to reproduce a particular period or style, wood choice is one of the main concerns. Mission pieces, for example, were traditionally made of solid oak—a material that accounts for much of the character of this style. To reproduce the Mission style, oak is the obvious choice but not necessarily the only option. If you choose to build in another wood, it should be for a sound reason. Woods close to oak in color and grain pattern, such as ash or

Designing
Tapers

A shallow taper on one side (left) affords an elegant line without sacrificing the look of strength. Adjacent sides can be tapered to produce a light appearance (middle). Or opposite sides can be tapered (right) and the legs inlaid to achieve a period look.

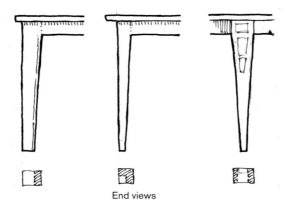

End views

Feet Must
Fit the Style

Adding a foot to a table leg can help ground a piece. The pad foot (right) and bun foot (middle) are inappropriate for this Federal-style leg from the late 18th century. This design calls for a simpler foot (left), lightening the piece and making the table appear to float.

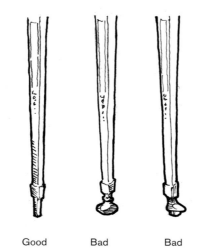

Good   Bad   Bad

Details Must
Work Together

The leg on the far right is composed of disparate elements—a turned fret pattern, poorly proportioned foot, and bun head—that fail even though they are all from the same (mahogany) period. The leg on the left is modified for a more successful design: a substantial square foot on a simple fluted leg with an appropriate head.

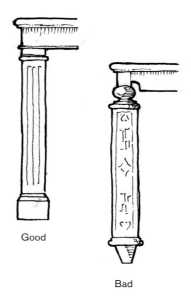

Good

Bad

elm, may complement the design. Or you may want to soften the heavy look of this style by altering the scale or by building in a lighter wood like cherry, but you should realize that you're no longer building a period piece.

A table may also have the appearance of being solidly grounded, or it may take on a more delicate look. A leg that rests on a solid base and is joined to other legs by low rails or stretchers gives the appearance of sturdiness. Using a substantial foot at the end of a leg also makes a table appear balanced and solid. A tapered leg, whether plain, square or turned, will give the look of delicacy, even of floating. This idea can be developed further by altering the form of the taper: for example, tapering a square leg on one, two, three, or four sides.

A classically designed leg in the Federal style might be more appropriate for tables requiring a dignified appearance. Conference tables, library tables, or formal dining tables often need this sense of sobriety. But there is also room to be playful. Flights of fancy embodied in curvilinear pieces, both regular and free-form, can transform an ordinary table into a contemporary expression of individuality.

Whatever style you choose, make sure that it is environmentally compatible. This simply means that you must take the surroundings into account—either locally, in terms of the pieces directly around it, or globally, in terms of the larger surroundings in which the piece will live. Sometimes, of course, none of this is known to the maker, and you can do no more than aim to be as true as possible to the piece's own character—square legs on square tables, for example.

Designing legs that are appropriate to a particular era requires that you recognize the design parameters underlying the style. Knowing how particular styles developed, the features and techniques that were used, and the characteristics the builder was after will help you design legs that are comfortable and right on any given table. It will also steer you away from infelicitous mistakes like trying to graft Jacobean legs onto a Chippendale piece.

From Gothic to Contemporary: A Brief History of Legs

What follows is a chronological look at some of the major periods of Western furniture. It should provide not only a broad outline of the more important styles but also tell you what to look for when you're trying to decide whether a particular leg detail will be appropriate for the situation at hand.

Gothic/medieval

Apart from various esoteric pieces from antiquity, such as Egyptian chairs found in pyramid tombs and Greek and Roman furniture known primarily from artistic representations, furniture from the 14th and 15th centuries constitutes the first period from which actual examples are readily found. These were vigorous, if not violent, times, and the furniture that remains is, appropriately enough, decidedly sturdy, relying largely on heavy hardwoods such as oak and chestnut.

Early tables often were placed upon trestles for mobility. These "proto-legs'" were often ecclesiastical in character. They were sometimes carved with graceful Gothic tracery, using intersecting circles to form pointed arches and other geometrically inspired shapes. More commonly, they consisted of pairs of simple slabs, occasionally made single and supported by one broad foot.

The age of oak

As more permanence was achieved, "joined" tables became common in the 16th century. Dining tables were invariably massive, with large legs typically joined near their bottoms by sturdy stretchers that served not only to strengthen the legs but also to provide a place to rest one's foot—off a drafty and perhaps dirty stone floor.

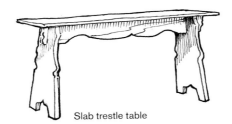

Slab trestle table

Heavy turned and carved legs with bottom stretchers (late 16th century)

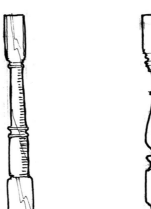

Simple turned leg

17th-century turned leg

"Country pine" turned kitchen table leg

Early types employed a central stretcher connected to pairs of legs. This stretcher system has the advantage of providing plenty of space for the sitter's legs.

Square legs were frequently chamfered and cusped, with square stretchers mortised into them and secured with pegs. Turned legs range from basic cylinders with simple rings and square ends to those with exaggerated shapes sumptuously carved and displaying a variety of motifs—from acanthus leaves to satyr heads.

Contemporary uses for legs made in this style might include a single turned and carved leg for a round dining table or simpler versions of the turned variety with square ends used in a kitchen or on a work table—as seen in much so-called "English country pine."

Seventeenth-century walnut

By the 17th century, tables—from large dining tables to smaller altar or writing tables—became more delicate and fanciful. Their legs were no longer merely

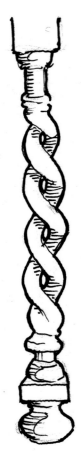

Double-spiral twist leg

17th-century spiral twist leg with curved stretcher

straight but often curved and exhibiting pronounced turned elements—spirals, double twists, cups, and a variety of inlay. Stretchers connecting the legs also became more varied, with lighter, curved pieces replacing the heavy, structural members found on earlier tables. There is a distinct Renaissance influence in much of the carving of this period.

While it is possible to divide the period into numerous categories that vary widely from one to another—such as Jacobean in Europe and Pilgrim Century furniture in America—legs from this period were generally more sophisticated and refined than those from the Gothic/medieval and oak periods. At the same time, the legs were also more inventive and decorated than those of the succeeding periods. The 17th century

probably presents the contemporary designer with more choices than any other period, especially if he or she is not constrained by matching or harmonizing the piece with any other furniture or a particular surrounding. While the construction tends to be traditional, the shape, ornamentation, and material are susceptible to infinite invention, as a visit to any museum with tables from this period will demonstrate.

Queen Anne walnut

At the beginning of the 18th century, a stylistic reaction to earlier exuberance set in. The so-called Queen Anne style—which lasted much longer than Queen Anne's actual reign—was typified by restraint and a lessening of ornament. More attention was paid to purity of line and elegance of design, and this was particularly typified by the Queen Anne cabriole leg with pad foot and later the ball-and-claw foot, both with minimal carving.

This was the beginning of the classic 18th-century style of furniture, which came to be known in Britain as the Georgian period. In America this period was represented by such luminaries as Thomas

Legs Marching Across Time

A survey of tables, from Gothic to present times, shows a progression from simple to ornate and, in some cases, back to simple again.

From left to right: **trestle table** made of pine and ash in a medieval design; **long joined table** in red oak with classically turned legs and a carved guilloche border on the apron; **"thousand-leg" table** made of walnut, yellow pine and white pine, complete with gatelegs and numerous turnings.

Gothic

Affleck and other Philadelphia cabinet-makers. Many other sought-after makers, such as the Goddards and Townsends of Newport, R.I., were recasting design. These men based their designs on classical paradigms and proportions derived from Greek and Roman architecture.

If you wish to design in this style, it is important to learn something about the underlying proportional system that dictates fundamentals—height-to-width ratios, for instance. Start by paying close attention to the wealth of published material that is available on this period.

Mahogany furniture

As the 18th century wore on, there was a return to ornamentation, and by the time of Chippendale, table legs were once again heavily carved with lions' feet, fretwork, flutes, and all manner of brackets.

Although successful designs in this style require at least a passing awareness of basic underlying design principles, there are a host of details that identify separate varieties. Often, randomly mixing and matching in an attempt to reproduce the general flavor of this period fails and simply looks silly.

Correct Details Are No Substitute for Overall Balance

The cabriole leg at far right is composed of congruous details but designed with no attention to the overall form. Not understanding or being sensitive to the underlying proportional rationale, the builder creates a leg that is mis-shapen and unhappy. The leg does little to give the table a feeling of comfortable support (it looks like it might easily break) or appropriate elegance. Poorly understood period pieces look silly, but overall form is even more important with contemporary pieces, where the design vocabulary is much more relaxed.

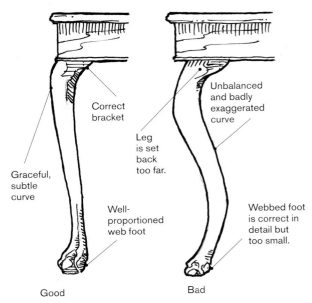

Correct bracket

Graceful, subtle curve

Well-proportioned web foot

Good

Unbalanced and badly exaggerated curve

Leg is set back too far.

Webbed foot is correct in detail but too small.

Bad

Card table with cabriole legs and pad feet

Age of Oak

17th-Century Walnut

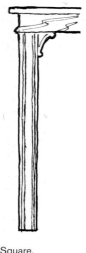

Square,
reeded leg

Cluster
fretwork leg

Volute foot
on carved
cabriole leg

Chippendale silver
table (with gallery)

But if you choose the details carefully—a particular foot, a certain stretcher type, an overall shape or proportion—and keep an eye on overall balance, both in terms of weight (as implied by the actual size and dimensions of various parts) and form (as constituted by color, wood species, and ornamentation, such as carving or inlay), you can produce something new and exciting from ideas that have stood the test of time.

The important thing is to avoid replicating a particular style exactly—such as a New York side table from 1790—and, from a lack of familiarity, giving it something incongruous, such as a Boston foot. Details should always be subservient to the whole. However much as a particular detail may appeal to you, do not hesitate to alter or adjust it appropriately for the sake of the design as a whole.

Late 18th century

By the end of the 18th century, designers such as Robert and James Adam, Thomas Sheraton, and George Hepplewhite had introduced even more classical elements:

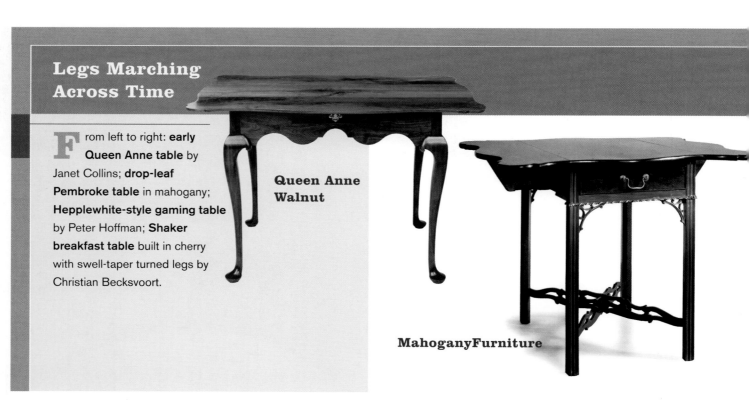

Legs Marching Across Time

From left to right: **early Queen Anne table** by Janet Collins; **drop-leaf Pembroke table** in mahogany; **Hepplewhite-style gaming table** by Peter Hoffman; **Shaker breakfast table** built in cherry with swell-taper turned legs by Christian Becksvoort.

Queen Anne Walnut

MahoganyFurniture

stretcherless tapered legs; architectural details such as classically inspired spandrels, pilasters and fluting; and a great deal of inlay in the form of shells, urns, stringing, and banding. This was possible, of course, because cabinetmaking techniques—based mainly on veneered construction—had largely overtaken the older forms of solid-wood joinery.

Realizing this, you can avoid using these techniques on legs destined for a table designed in an earlier style. Put another way, it is invariably better to restrict your design ideas to those elements that go hand-in-hand with the type of construction being employed.

Nineteenth century

In the 19th century, the general introduction of powered machinery and the large-scale production of furniture began to affect the one-man/several-apprentice shops that had previously been the norm. It was also a period given to stylistic revivals. Consequently, there are as many distinct forms, fads, styles, and schools originating from this period as from practically all preceding centuries.

A close look at some of these styles can be instructive. To start with, the very popular Shaker style is well known as a model of simplicity and unadorned sobriety. Construction is honest and straightforward. Very little is added that does not have an essential structural purpose. This demand for functional furniture results in simple turned or plainly tapered legs sufficient for the job of supporting the table. Legs were usually made from the most practical material at hand, eschewing the use of rare and exotic species that might require additional work. Try using these principles by designing a leg that represents the minimum possible construction for sufficient support.

In sharp contrast to Shaker simplicity was mass-produced Victorian furniture, which sought to embody whatever fantastic element was the fashion of the day. This included applied veneer pieces, pressed patterns, gilded incised designs, spindled galleries, machine fluting, and coarse carving

Hepplewhite/Sheraton-style table with stretcherless legs that are tapered and inlaid.

Late 18th Century

19th Century

Overall Form Is More Important than Correctness of Detail

This table is composed of elements—such as the fretwork skirt, heavily carved knees and biche (deer) feet—that are all from different periods, making the table stylistically incorrect. But the design works because the overall form is graceful, and the various components make structural sense.

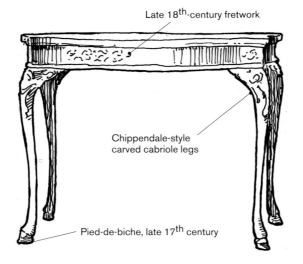

Late 18th-century fretwork

Chippendale-style carved cabriole legs

Pied-de-biche, late 17th century

Shaker table: absolute simplicity

(often on two-dimensionally shaped members). One well-known example of revivalist fashion is furniture inspired by the designer Charles Eastlake, who was responsible for introducing the principles of the English design reform movement to America. Originally conceived as a reaction against the melodramatic red plush and extravagant furniture of midcentury, this resulted in a series of more simplified styles drawing upon earlier models, such as Modern Gothic and Queen Anne Revival.

Today, much of this furniture can seem excessively busy, but it serves the contemporary designer as a model of how earlier elements can be reinterpreted. Although some of the results may be seen as a travesty

of the pieces that inspired them, it is instructive to observe how they present a coherent identity when reinterpreted and incorporated into new work. This is another important idea to bear in mind: A well-designed leg—of whatever style—will stand on its own merits as long as you have fulfilled the structural requirements and have conceived the leg and the table as a whole.

Twentieth-century contemporary

With the arrival of the 20th century, several factors converged to create a landscape that was, at least superficially, even more puzzling for the designer. On one hand, the 19th century's infatuation with rediscovering old styles—from Gothic to Turkish—had produced an almost limitless number of confusing design ideas. On the other hand, there was a severe reaction to everything overly ornamented and complicated. The Arts and Crafts movement's return to simple craftsmanship—starting with designers such as William Morris and continuing across the Atlantic to people such as Gustav Stickley in upstate New York—had produced, by comparison, a spartan and four-square approach that foreshadowed the later Bauhaus movement of the midcentury. Added to these diverse approaches, the increase of machinery, new methods of production and changing

Legs Marching Across Time

From left to right: **Wendell Castle's 1985 table, "Never Complain,"** made of purpleheart veneer, leather and copper; **maple end table** made by William Walker; **slab coffee table** designed and built by George Nakashima in the 1940s.

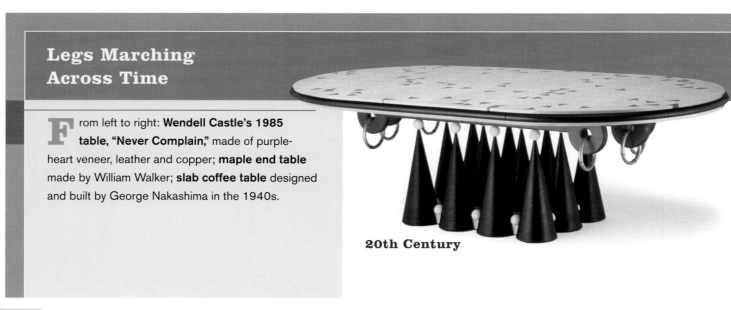

20th Century

market conditions (due, especially, to World Wars I and II) all provided an extremely fertile ground for a variety of new styles.

Some lines of development continued the simple approach. Out of the Arts and Crafts movement came designers concerned with honesty, simplicity, and good workmanship. People such as Edward Barnsley, Allan Peters and even James Krenov have continued to embody this approach. At the other end of the design spectrum, a purely artistic spirit produced the fluid and nature-inspired shapes of the Art Nouveau movement, which merged with the increasingly modern ideas of the Art Deco movement. This resulted in the exciting use of new and different materials, including sharkskin, aluminum and laminates. Designers such as Jacques-Emile Ruhlmann and Wendell Castle have expanded our ideas of what can be achieved if the constraints of traditionalism are laid aside.

More recently there has been a flowering of talented new designers produced by a renewed interest in high-quality woodworking. There are now schools in Britain and America where the making of well-constructed and well-designed furniture—both contemporary and traditional—is taught.

The result has been a century with more choices than ever for the designer. It would seem that anything goes. But for all of the apparent variety, the fundamentals of good design remain; overall harmony, structural sufficiency, and balance cannot be ignored.

James Krenov's furniture may be well-known for its sensitive and delicate attention to overall harmony of color and grain, George Nakashima can be appreciated for his use of natural forms, and the Memphis style may stand out by virtue of its uncompromising and radical approach to color and geometrics, but all three of these superficially different approaches succeed because their fundamental concern is with the given piece as a balanced whole. The successful and varied elements of earlier periods are still important and endlessly instructional.

No matter what construction methods you use, no matter what style you prefer, strive always to design a leg that bears the lessons of the past in mind. Remember, above all, to design legs that are an integral part of the whole piece.

GRAHAM BLACKBURN is a furniture maker, illustrator, author and the publisher of Blackburn Books in Woodstock, N.Y.

Victorian table leg is an eclectic mix of Gothic, Tudor, and Romanesque.

1920s Art Deco (Ruhlmann table)

Krenov-style silver table

Credits

The articles in this book appeared in the following issues of *Fine Woodworking*:

p. 20: Building in the Language of Greene and Greene by Thomas Hugh Stangeland, issue 106. Photos on pp. 20–21 by Gregg Krogstad; photos on pp. 22–24 by Jonathan Binzen, courtesy *Fine Woodworking*, © The Taunton Press, Inc.; Drawings p. 27 by Maria Meleschnig.

p. 28: Elements of the Shaker Style by Christian Becksvoort, issue 131. Photos on pp. 29 and 32 by Scott Phillips, courtesy *Fine Woodworking*, © The Taunton Press, Inc. Furniture courtesy Hancock Shaker Village, Pittsfield, MA.; Drawings on pp. 32–33 by Michael Gellatly.

p. 34: Furniture Design: The Four Objectives by Mike Dunbar, issue 148. Photo on p. 36 (top right) by Boyd Hagen, courtesy *Fine Woodworking*, © The Taunton Press, Inc.; Photo on p. 36 (bottom left) © Gene Sasse.

p. 37: Designing Furniture: A Survival Guide, issue 156. Photos on pp. 37 and 39 by Asa Christiana, courtesy *Fine Woodworking*, © The Taunton Press, Inc.; Drawings on p. 38 by Michael Pekovich.

p. 41: Building Without Plans by Craig Vandall Stevens, issue 142. Photos on pp. 41–45 by Jonathan Binzen, courtesy *Fine Woodworking*, © The Taunton Press, Inc. Photos on p. 46 (left) by Jonathan Binzen, courtesy *Fine Woodworking*, © The Taunton Press, Inc.; (right) © Craig Stevens.

p. 47: Creating Working Drawings by Jim Tolpin, issue 101. Photos

on pp. 47–48 by Vincent Laurence, courtesy *Fine Woodworking*, © The Taunton Press, Inc.

p. 53: Drafting Tools by Philip C. Lowe, issue 161. Photos on p. 56–58 by Asa Christiana, courtesy *Fine Woodworking*, © The Taunton Press, Inc.

p. 60: Models Help Projects Succeed by Jan Zaitlin, issue 111. Photos on pp. 60–64 by William Sampson, courtesy *Fine Woodworking*, © The Taunton Press, Inc.

p. 65: Organize Your Projects by Jan Tolpin, issue 103. Photos on pp. 65–68 by Vincent Laurence, courtesy *Fine Woodworking*, © The Taunton Press, Inc.

p. 71: A Drafting Table for Shop or Home by Cameron Russell, issue 123. Photos on pp. 74–76 by William Duckworth, courtesy *Fine Woodworking*, © The Taunton Press, Inc.

p. 77: Doors Make the Difference by Christian Becksvoort, issue 106. Photos on pp. 77–80 © Christian Becksvoort.

p. 82: Joining Legs to Aprons by Garrett Hack, issue 161. Photos on pp. 85–87 by William Duckworth, courtesy *Fine Woodworking*, © The Taunton Press, Inc.; Drawings on p. 88 by Bob La Pointe.

p. 89: Graduated Drawers by Christian Becksvoort, issue 142. Drawings by Vince Babak.

p. 91: Exposing Your Back Side by Christian Becksvoort, issue 103. Cabinet on p. 91 built by John Thoe of Seattle, Wash. Photos on

pp. 91 and 93 by Alec Waters, courtesy *Fine Woodworking*, © The Taunton Press, Inc. Drawings on p.92 by Matthew Wells; Photo on p.94 © Christian Becksvoort.

p. 95: Making Dining Tables That Work by Peter Tischler, issue 107. Photos on pp. 95–98 by Alec Waters, courtesy *Fine Woodworking*, © The Taunton Press, Inc.

p. 99: Large-Case Construction Strategies by Bruce Cohen, issue 131. Photos on pp. 99–103 by Strother Purdy, courtesy *Fine Woodworking*, © The Taunton Press, Inc.

p. 104: Designing a Chest of Drawers by Garrett Hack, issue 151. Photos on pp. 106–109 by John Sheldon, © Garrett Hack; Drawing on p. 107 by Vince Babak.

p. 110: Sideboard Strategies by Will Neptune, issue 138. Photo on p. 110 by Scott Phillips, © The Taunton Press, Inc.; all other photos by Michael Pekovich, courtesy *Fine Woodworking*, © The Taunton Press, Inc. Drawings by Bob La Pointe.

p. 120: Designing on the Go: A Coffe Table Takes Shape by Peter Turner, issue 128. Photos by Scott Gibson, © The Taunton Press, Inc., except photos on pp. 120–121 © Pete Macomber and photo on p. 122 © Dennis and Diane Griggs. Drawings by Vince Babak.

p. 125: Where the Furniture Meets the Floor by Mario Rodriguez, issue 135. Photos by Jonathan Binzen, courtesy *Fine Woodworking*, © The Taunton Press, Inc., except photos on pp. 125, 126 (lower

left), 127 (lower right), 129, 131 by Michael Pekovich, courtesy *Fine Woodworking*, © The Taunton Press, Inc. Drawings by Vince Babak.

p. 133: Dressing Up a Basic Box by Roger Holmes, issue 152. Photos by Michael Farrell, courtesy *Fine Woodworking*, © The Taunton Press, Inc. Drawings by Vince Babak.

p. 136: Going Over Edges by Will Neptune, issue 132. Photos by Lance Patterson, courtesy *Fine Woodworking*, © The Taunton Press, Inc. Drawings by Vince Babak.

p. 142: Designing Table Legs by Graham Blackburn, issue 139. Photo on p. 146 © E. Irving Blomstrann, courtesy of The Wadsworth Antheneum; Photos on

p. 147 courtesy of The Wadsworth Antheneum; photo on p. 148 (bottom left) © Lance Patterson, courtesy of North Bennet Street School and p. 148 (bottom right) © E. Irving Blomstrann, courtesy of The Wadsworth Antheneum; photo on p. 149 (bottom left) © Lance Patterson, courtesy of North Bennet Street School and

p. 149 (bottom right) © Christian Becksvoort; photo on p. 150 © Mark Haven, courtesy of Wendell Castle, Inc.; photo on

p. 151 (bottom left) © Chris Eden and p. 151 (bottom right) © George Erml, courtesy of George Nakashima. Drawings by Graham Blackburn.

Index